NATIONAL GEOGRAPHIC

book of nature poetry

With favorites from Langston Hughes, Naomi Shihab Nye, Billy Collins, and more

More than 200 poems with photographs that *float*, ZOOM, and bloom!

Edited by J. Patrick Lewis, former U.S. Children's Poet Laureate

NATIONAL GEOGRAPHIC
WASHINGTON, D.C.

FRONT COVER: NORTHERN LIGHTS, NORTHWEST TERRITORIES, CANADA;
BACK COVER: BANDED DEMOISELLE; CASE COVER: (FRONT) PACIFIC
CHORUS FROG IN DAHLIA (BACK) FALL MAPLE LEAVES

J. PATRICK LEWIS HAS WRITTEN MORE THAN 95 PICTURE AND POETRY BOOKS FOR YOUNG READERS. IN 2011 HE WAS APPOINTED U.S. CHILDREN'S POET LAUREATE, AND WAS GIVEN THE NATIONAL COUNCIL OF TEACHERS OF ENGLISH AWARD FOR EXCELLENCE IN POETRY FOR CHILDREN.

To poets, nature, and nature poets everywhere. —JPL

HENRY DAVID THOREAU was one of America's truly Big Thinkers on a little pond—Walden Pond. It was there in 1853, in a self-built cabin not far from his Massachusetts family home, that he wrote: "I have a room all to myself; it is nature."

From his tucked-away cottage, Thoreau produced some of the most profound thoughts on Mother Nature. But poets from centuries past rarely wrote about the more exotic natural wonders. They never saw them, never knew they existed. Many of the most fascinating phenomena that we often take for granted today—thanks to the convenience of travel, books, or photographs—were seldom brought to the attention of the classical poets.

How would William Shakespeare or John Keats have described in a poem the grandeur of the Grand Canyon? One can only imagine Emily Dickinson, transported to the scene, painting on an easel built of words a picture of an Asian tsunami or an African drought. What immortal verse might William Wordsworth have written after a day's walk in the Amazon rain forest instead of the English countryside?

What picture would Kobayashi Issa or Li Po paint after a submersible dive to the ocean deep?

And yet a poet does not have to *be* there! You needn't leave your chair to write a poem about the wilder shores of creation. A book is your ticket to ride; a photograph is rapid transit to the brain. What kind of poem would you write if all you had in front of you was an image, like one of the breathtaking pictures in the *Book of Nature Poetry* you are now holding?

Better yet, let your eyes be your camera, taking incredible pictures your brain will thank you for. Get up and go there! Explore the woods, a cave; climb a mountain; go scuba diving; or simply make a friend of a grasshopper in a field on a windy summer day. You might even imagine you *are* that dragonfly trying to escape a swift, or a lucky salmon that has wiggled through the legs of a grizzly bear.

Travel by photograph or on foot, but go quickly before nature disappears. Every day more than 70 animals, plants, or other living things, like fungi, roots, and molds, vanish forever. The *Book of Nature Poetry* seeks to capture the ever changing nature of nature, so that gone is not forgotten. Besides, when more of us care for nature, more can help save it.

However and wherever you greet the world outside your window, listen again to Mr. Thoreau for the last and best words of advice:

"It's not what you look at that matters. It's what you see."

—J. Patrick Lewis,
former U.S. Children's Poet Laureate

The Thing Is the Thing Is Green

The thing is the thing is green and the green is green and by green I mean real mean green. I mean electric-eel green, alligator, iguana, anaconda green. I mean this thing has got all things green. It's got green turtles in turtle-green ponds and grasshoppers springing from groomed-green lawns and a green tree frog on a girl's left arm. It's got dark and dangerous greens. Greens you've never even seen greens. Ocean floor greens. Tornado sky greens. Tiger's eye greens. Eat-your-broccoli greens. Watermelons sparkling in the sun greens. Way beyond evergreen, this thing leaves green geckos on green leaves feeling green and green moths in the green dark and preying mantises on their thin green knees. It's a great and gorgeous green a light-bright-just-right-watch-it-grow-it-says-go shade of green. Have you guessed yet? Do you need another clue? Think rolling waves of grain green. Thick arms of vines climbing tall green trees. Mountains and mountains of green billions of waves reaching out of dark green seas all wrapped in one green ball and hung, an ornament in the sky. What a thing it must be to see the whole green thing floating by. It's true. The thing is the thing is green . . .

except when it's blue.

—Peggy Gifford

EARTH AS SEEN FROM SPACE

THE WONDER OF
NAT

URE

The Delight Song of Tsoai-talee

I am a feather on the bright sky
I am the blue horse that runs in the plain
I am the fish that rolls, shining, in the water
I am the shadow that follows a child
I am the evening light, the lustre of meadows
I am an eagle playing with the wind
I am a cluster of bright beads
I am the farthest star
I am the cold of the dawn
I am the roaring of the rain
I am the glitter on the crust of the snow
I am the long track of the moon in a lake
I am a flame of four colors
I am a deer standing away in the dusk
I am a field of sumac and the pomme blanche
I am an angle of geese in the winter sky
I am the hunger of a young wolf
I am the whole dream of these things

You see, I am alive, I am alive
I stand in good relation to the earth
I stand in good relation to the gods
I stand in good relation to all that is beautiful
I stand in good relation to the daughter of Tsen-tainte
You see, I am alive, I am alive

—N. Scott Momaday

from Childe Harold's Pilgrimage

There is a pleasure in the pathless woods,
There is a rapture on the lonely shore,
There is society where none intrudes,
By the deep Sea, and music in its roar:
I love not Man the less, but Nature more.

—*George Gordon, Lord Byron*

PESCADERO STATE BEACH, CALIFORNIA, U.S.A.

To Look at Any Thing

To look at any thing,
If you would know that thing,
You must look at it long:
To look at this green and say
"I have seen spring in these
Woods," will not do—you must
Be the thing you see:
You must be the dark snakes of
Stems and ferny plumes of leaves,
You must enter in
To the small silences between
The leaves,
You must take your time
And touch the very peace
They issue from.

—John Moffitt

Perseverance

I shall look at the grass
Till I obtain the degree
Of Doctor of Grass.

I shall look at the clouds
Till I become a Master
Of Clouds.

I shall walk beside the smoke
Till out of shame
The smoke returns to the flame
Of its beginning.

I shall walk beside all things
Till all things
Come to know me.

—Marin Sorescu

*Translated by D. J. Enright
and Joana Russell-Gebbett*

Manna

Everywhere, *everywhere*, snow sifting down,
a world becoming white, no more sounds,
no longer possible to find the heart of the day,
the sun is gone, the sky is nowhere, and of all
I wanted in life—so be it—whatever it is
that brought me here, chance, fortune, whatever
blessing each flake of snow is the hint of, I am
grateful. I bear witness, I hold out my arms,
palms up, I know it is impossible to hold
for long what we love of the world, but look
at me, is it foolish, shameful, arrogant to say this,
see how the snow drifts down, look how happy
I am.

—Joseph Stroud

Leisure

What is this life if, full of care,
We have no time to stand and stare.

No time to stand beneath the boughs
And stare as long as sheep or cows.

No time to see, when woods we pass,
Where squirrels hide their nuts in grass.

No time to see, in broad daylight,
Streams full of stars, like skies at night.

No time to turn at Beauty's glance,
And watch her feet, how they can dance.

No time to wait till her mouth can
Enrich that smile her eyes began.

A poor life this if, full of care,
We have no time to stand and stare.

—*W. H. Davies*

ELWHA RIVER, WASHINGTON, U.S.A.

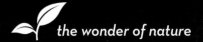

Four Haiku

I
Don't worry, spiders,
I keep house
casually.

II
How *much*
are you enjoying yourself,
tiger moth?

III
In this world
we walk on the roof of hell,
gazing at flowers.

IV
Even with insects—
some can sing,
some can't.

—*Kobayashi Issa*

Translated by Robert Hass

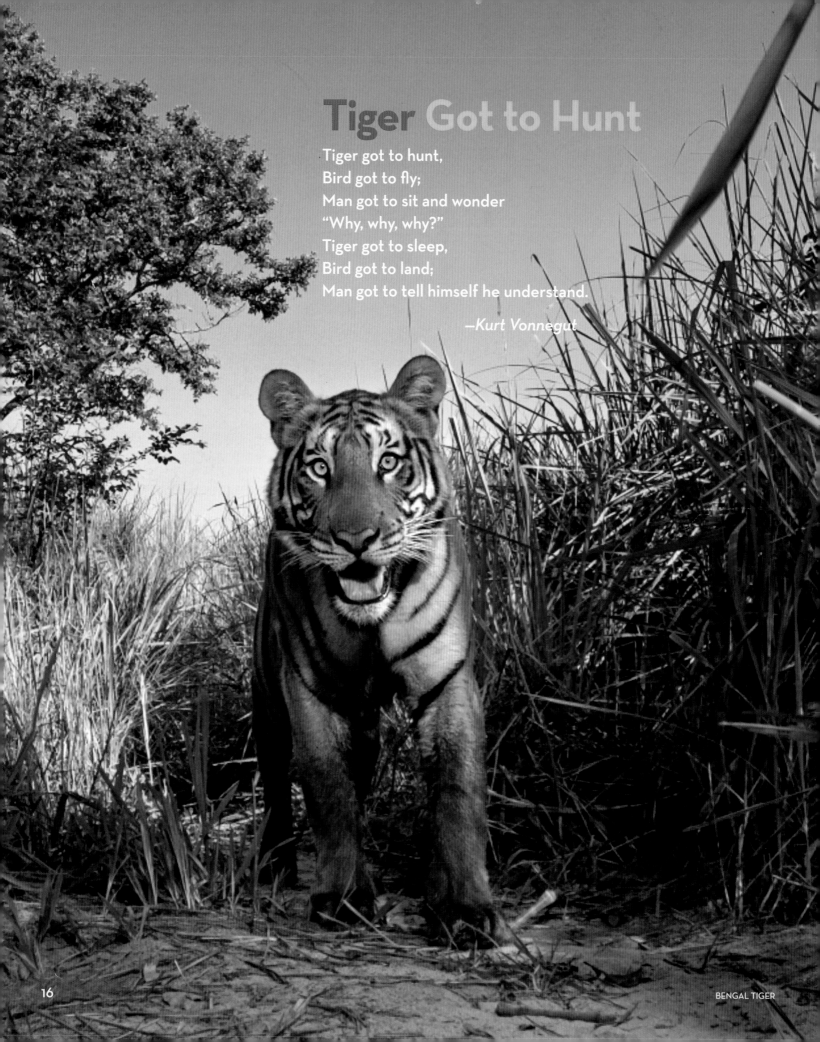

Tiger Got to Hunt

Tiger got to hunt,
Bird got to fly;
Man got to sit and wonder
"Why, why, why?"
Tiger got to sleep,
Bird got to land;
Man got to tell himself he understand.

—*Kurt Vonnegut*

16

BENGAL TIGER

BIRCH LEAVES

"Nature"
Is What We See

"Nature" is what we see—
The Hill—the Afternoon—
Squirrel—Eclipse—the Bumble bee—
Nay—Nature is Heaven—
Nature is what we hear—
The Bobolink—the Sea—
Thunder—the Cricket—

Nay—Nature is Harmony—
Nature is what we know—
Yet have no art to say—
So impotent Our Wisdom is
To her Simplicity.

—*Emily Dickinson*

RETURN

These woods were young when, setting out from home,
I navigated coasts and coated plains
toward lands and legends, all of them unknown.
But now I walk familiar roads again,
more tired than before, but heartbeat high
on seeing well-worn moss and well-known stone
and finding in the leaves that frame the sky,
the light unchanged, although the trees have grown.

—*Paige Towler*

WOODS, GOUGANE BARRA, IRELAND

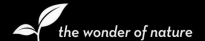

Four Haiku

I
How admirable!
to see lightning and not think
life is fleeting.

II
First winter rain—
even the monkey
seems to want a raincoat.

III
Winter solitude—
in a world of one color
the sound of wind.

IV
What fish feel,
birds feel, I don't know—
the year ending.

—*Matsuo Basho*

Translated by Robert Hass

The Morns Are Meeker Than They Were

The morns are meeker than they were,
The nuts are getting brown;
The berry's cheek is plumper,
The rose is out of town.

The maple wears a gayer scarf;
The field a scarlet gown.
Lest I should be old-fashioned,
I'll put a trinket on.

—*Emily Dickinson*

The Peace of Wild Things

When despair for the world grows in me
and I wake in the night at the least sound
in fear of what my life and my children's lives may be,
I go and lie down where the wood drake
rests in his beauty on the water, and the great heron feeds.
I come into the peace of wild things
who do not tax their lives with forethought
of grief. I come into the presence of still water.
And I feel above me the day-blind stars
waiting with their light. For a time
I rest in the grace of the world, and am free.

—*Wendell Berry*

GREAT BLUE HERON

IN THE

SEAGULLS, SAMUT PRAKAN, THAILAND

SKy

Changing of the Guard

In their twice-a-day meeting
Sun and moon exchange
The same greeting,
"Hello," "Goodbye."
With a nod of the head,
One's off to work,
One's off to bed.

—Charles Waters

from Night

The sun descending in the west,
The evening star does shine;
The birds are silent in their nest,
And I must seek for mine.
The moon, like a flower
In heaven's high bower,
With silent delight,
Sits and smiles on the night.

—William Blake

SEASTACKS, OLYMPIC NATIONAL PARK, WASHINGTON, U.S.A.

Welcome to the Night

To all of you who crawl and creep,
who buzz and chirp and hoot and peep,
who wake at dusk and throw off sleep:
Welcome to the night.

To you who make the forest sing,
who dip and dodge on silent wing,
who flutter, hover, clasp, and cling:
Welcome to the night!

Come feel the cool and shadowed breeze,
come smell your way among the trees,
come touch rough bark and leathered leaves:
Welcome to the night.

The night's a sea of dappled dark,
the night's a feast of sound and spark,
the night's a wild, enchanted park.
Welcome to the night!

—Joyce Sidman

Old Man Moon

The moon is very, very old.
The reason why is clear—
he gets a birthday once a month,
instead of once a year.

—Aileen Fisher

The Man
in the mOOn

He used to frighten me in the nights of childhood,
the wide adult face, enormous, stern, aloft.
I could not imagine such loneliness, such coldness.

But tonight as I drive home over these hilly roads
I see him sinking behind stands of winter trees
and rising again to show his familiar face.

And when he comes into full view over open fields
he looks like a young man who has fallen in love
with the dark earth,

a pale bachelor, well-groomed and full of melancholy,
his round mouth open
as if he had just broken into song.

—Billy Collins

Write About a Radish

Write about a radish
too many people write about the moon.

The night is black
the stars are small and high
the clock unwinds its ever-ticking tune
hills gleam dimly
distant nighthawks cry.
A radish rises in the waiting sky.

—Karla Kuskin

The **Aged Sun**

Whether our star, the sun, grows old
By turning into liquid gold

And dripping down invisible space
To some celestial fireplace,

Expands, like science says it must,
And turns its planets into dust,

Or simply ups and disappears
Like some ascending-ending spheres,

I do not think it matters much.
Great things collapse, depart, lose touch

When slow time reckons they are done—
And so it will be with the sun.

—Anonymous

 *in the sky*

Two Falling Flakes

Two falling flakes by chance did meet,

Lived happily ever after

Till they hit the street.

—*Douglas Florian*

GEESE IN NEW ENGLAND, U.S.A.

Snow

In the gloom of whiteness,
In the great silence of snow,
A child was sighing
And bitterly saying: "Oh,
They have killed a white bird up there on her nest,
The down is fluttering from her breast!"
And still it fell through that dusky brightness
On the child crying for the bird of the snow.

—*Edward Thomas*

Looking Through Space

If people are living
on Venus and Mars
and looking through space
at the planets and stars,
I wonder if Earth
seems a queer sort of thing,
with whiteness in winter
and greenness in spring.

—Aileen Fisher

EARTH'S ATMOSPHERE AS SEEN FROM SPACE

Night Comes...

Night comes
leaking
out of the sky.

Stars come
peeking.

Moon comes
sneaking
silvery-sly.

Who is
shaking,
shivery-
quaking?

Who is afraid
of the night?

Not I.

—Beatrice Schenk de Regniers

A Baby-Sermon

The lightning and thunder
    They go and they come
But the stars and the stillness
    Are always at home.

—George Macdonald

MOUNT HOOD AND LOST LAKE, OREGON, U.S.A.

Stars

Stars, I have seen them fall,
    But when they drop and die
No star is lost at all
    From all the star-sown sky.
The toil of all that be
    Helps not the primal fault;
It rains into the sea,
    And still the sea is salt.

—*A. E. Housman*

When I Heard the Learn'd Astronomer

When I heard the learn'd astronomer,
When the proofs, the figures, were ranged in columns before me,
When I was shown the charts and diagrams, to add, divide, and measure them,
When I sitting heard the astronomer where he lectured with much applause in the
  lecture-room,
How soon unaccountable I became tired and sick,
Till rising and gliding out I wander'd off by myself,
In the mystical moist night-air, and from time to time,
Look'd up in perfect silence at the stars.

—*Walt Whitman*

SOUTH SISTER AND SPARKS LAKE, OREGON, U.S.A.

The **Opposite** of a **Cloud**

The opposite of a *cloud* could be
A white reflection in the sea,
Or a huge blueness in the air,
Caused by a cloud's not being there.

—*Richard Wilbur*

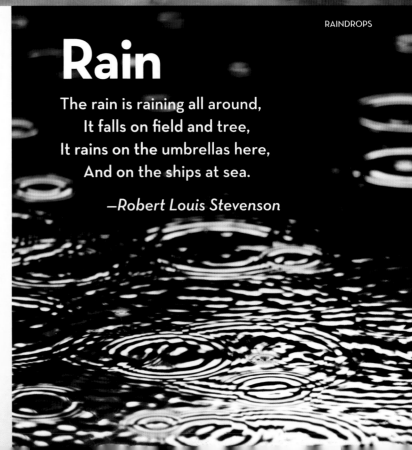

Rain

The rain is raining all around,
    It falls on field and tree,
It rains on the umbrellas here,
    And on the ships at sea.

—*Robert Louis Stevenson*

Windy Nights

Whenever the moon and stars are set,
   Whenever the wind is high,
All night long in the dark and wet,
   A man goes riding by.
Late in the night when the fires are out,
Why does he gallop and gallop about?

Whenever the trees are crying aloud,
   And ships are tossed at sea,
By, on the highway, low and loud,
   By at the gallop goes he.
By at the gallop he goes, and then
By he comes back at the gallop again.

—Robert Louis Stevenson

The Wind

The wind stood up and gave a shout.
He whistled on his fingers and
Kicked the withered leaves about
And thumped the branches with his hand
And said that he'd kill and kill,
And so he will and so he will.

—James Stephens

The Blue Between

Everyone watches clouds,
naming creatures they've seen.
I see the sky differently,
I see the blue between—

The blue woman tugging
her stubborn cloud across the sky.
The blue giraffe stretching
to nibble a cloud floating by.
A pod of dancing dolphins,
cloud oceans, cargo ships,
a boy twirling his cloud
around a thin blue fingertip.

In those smooth wide places,
I see a different scene
In those cloudless spaces,
I see the blue between.

—Kristine O'Connell George

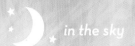

Icicles

Swell
and
grow,

put on
your
mighty show

this bitter-bold,
brutal-cold,
howling,
windy-wintry
day—

'cause
you
cannot
know

tomorrow's
tad
of sunshine prey

will
stalk

to
take

your
breath
away.

—*Lee Bennett Hopkins*

PONDEROSA PINE

San Francisco— Any Night

After Carl Sandburg

In the evening, the fog
billows in from the Bay.

It creeps
up the hills
the way a cat
sneaks up
on a bird at the feeder.

The fog, like the cat,
cannot long avoid detection.
Cresting the hilltops, it spills
down the streets,
a rolling blanket
of cold, grey mist.

Wear a coat.

Pull the collar close.

The bird may fly from the cat,
but no one can evade the fog.

—Kelly Ramsdell Fineman

The Sun and Fog

The Sun and Fog contested
The Government of Day—
The Sun took down his Yellow Whip
And drove the Fog away.

—Emily Dickinson

This Is My Rock

This is my rock,
And here I run
To steal the secret of the sun;

This is my rock,
And here come I
Before the night has swept the sky;

This is my rock,
This is the place
I meet the evening face to face.

—David McCord

SAN FRANCISCO, CALIFORNIA, U.S.A.

IN THE

GHOST CRAB, BAHIA, BRAZIL

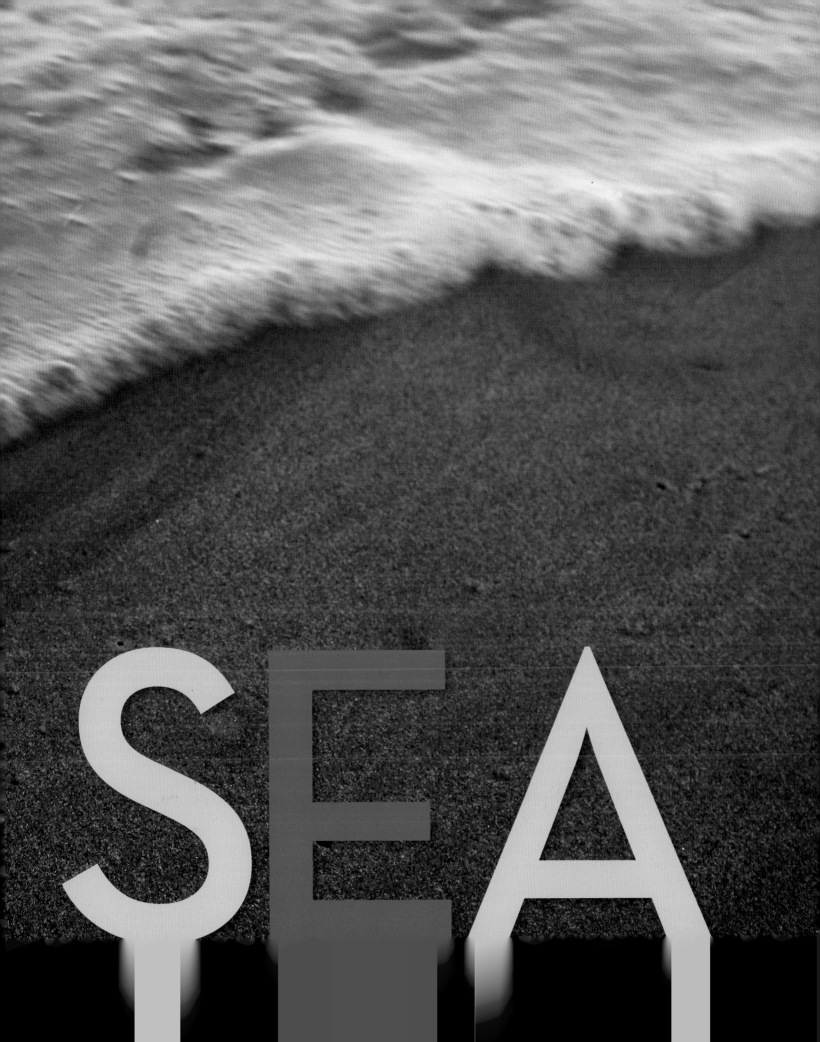

Tideline

Ocean draws on the sand
with trinkets of shell and stone,
the way I write on the sidewalk
with a stick of chalk at home.

She signs her name in letters
long and wavy and clear,
saying, "Don't forget me—

I was here,
　　wasss h e r e
　　　　wasssss h e r e . . ."

　　　　　　—Kate Coombs

By the Sea

The visitors strolling the sand
Look like they're willing to pay—
Though the ocean isn't selling
And the sun is closing for the day.

Still the walkers keep trolling
The purple shore, bags in hand,
And the sinking sun keeps tossing its gold
Recklessly on the sand.

We will scurry home with our haul tonight,
Dreaming of golden sand,
While the sea keeps throwing its treasures
Out as far and as fast as it can.

　　　　　　—Liz Rosenberg

At Seacliff Cottage

The breeze breezing me.
The sun sunning me.

The gulls arching.
The mist prancing over the waves.

The salted caramel spray
tanging the air.

The train whistling by,
low and wistful.

Some bird I've never heard before
wistfulling back.

A dragonfly
glinting by . . .

Who knew heaven could be rented?
Not I.

—Sonya Sones

Haiku

bass
picking bugs
off the moon

—Nick Virgilio

LARGEMOUTH BASS

The Negro
Speaks of Rivers

To W. E. B. DuBois

I've known rivers:
I've known rivers ancient as the world and older than the
flow of human blood in human veins.

My soul has grown deep like the rivers.

I bathed in the Euphrates when dawns were young.
I built my hut near the Congo and it lulled me to sleep.
I looked upon the Nile and raised the pyramids above it.
I heard the singing of the Mississippi when Abe Lincoln
        went down to New Orleans, and I've seen its muddy
        bosom turn all golden in the sunset.

I've known rivers:
Ancient, dusky rivers.

My soul has grown deep like the rivers.

—Langston Hughes

MISSISSIPPI RIVER, MISSISSIPPI, U.S.A.

The **Mississippi**

I heard it creep down from the north
at first in whispers, then it clapped
a river tune, and danced to steam—
blue tributaries bounding forth
from where geography had mapped
itself a continental stream.

I sat along the sandy bank,
like many a cane pole country boy,
to watch the waters lazing by.
Who cared if our red bobbers sank?
This mirror river of Illinois
reflected the enormous sky.

—Anonymous

Galápagos: Hood Island

Here's what I saw today:
a dazzling display of exotic wildlife
quietly sunbathing
side by side on the rocks:
Sally Lightfoot crabs, vivid as ripe tomatoes;
languid black lizards;
marine iguanas in dark brocade coats
now swathed
in turquoise and red;
seabirds swooping overhead;
pert yellow mockingbirds investigating the beach;
and sea lions of all sizes
snoozing, snuggling, swimming—
large eyes curious
velvety fur inviting
the forbidden touch of fingertips.
This is, I thought,
growing as fearlessly relaxed as the animals,
"The Peaceable Kingdom."

—*Bobbi Katz*

SALLY LIGHTFOOT CRAB, GALÁPAGOS, ECUADOR

NORTH SEA BLUE PEBBLES

St. Elmo's Fire

On the deck of the frigate
Sailors dropped to their knees.
As lightning flashed out of the west,
All eyes rose toward heaven.
Thunder drummed the skin of the sky.

The main masthead threw blue flames
While they whispered *spirit candles*
And crossed themselves—
St. Elmo's divine lantern
Come to light their way.

—Georgia Heard

Old Man Ocean

Old Man Ocean, how do you pound
 Smooth glass, rough stones round?
*Time and the tide and the wild waves rolling
Night and the wind and the long gray dawn.*

Old Man Ocean, what do you tell,
What do you sing in the empty shell?
*Fog and the storm and the long bell tolling,
Bones in the deep and the brave men gone.*

—Russell Hoban

Bigar
Cascade
Falls,
Romania

It's possible
    a frost giant
        tossed a
stony saucer
        across the river
and left a fossil
        faucet on
in a rocky posture of
        loss,
        awesome and
        austere,
still glossy with
        moss
and a docile
        jostling of waterfall
        floss.

—Steven Withrow

Flammable
Ice Bubbles

Alberta's Lake Abraham

Glass bubble bauble,
Classy high-priced diamond—
Each unreachable.

Pillowed clouds pinioned still
In the chilled lake's O'Keeffe sky—
A brilliant day.

Ice cracks. Dragon wakes.
His methane tongue of fire
Bursts from frozen depths.

—Richard Michelson

BIGAR CASCADE FALLS, ROMANIA

ICE BUBBLES, LAKE ABRAHAM, ALBERTA, CANADA

Lost Giant

A wetland spans a continent
across to such an elephant
as I, who knows the nomad bird
alone can fly him to the herd.

—*Mariel Bede*

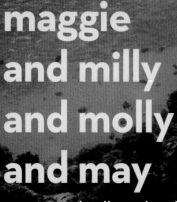

maggie
and milly
and molly
and may

maggie and milly and molly and may
went down to the beach(to play one day)

and maggie discovered a shell that sang
so sweetly she couldn't remember her troubles,and

milly befriended a stranded star
whose rays five languid fingers were;

and molly was chased by a horrible thing
which raced sideways while blowing bubbles:and

may came home with a smooth round stone
as small as a world and as large as alone.

For whatever we lose(like a you or a me)
it's always ourselves we find in the sea

—*e. e. cummings*

BLUE SEA STAR AND BAITFISH

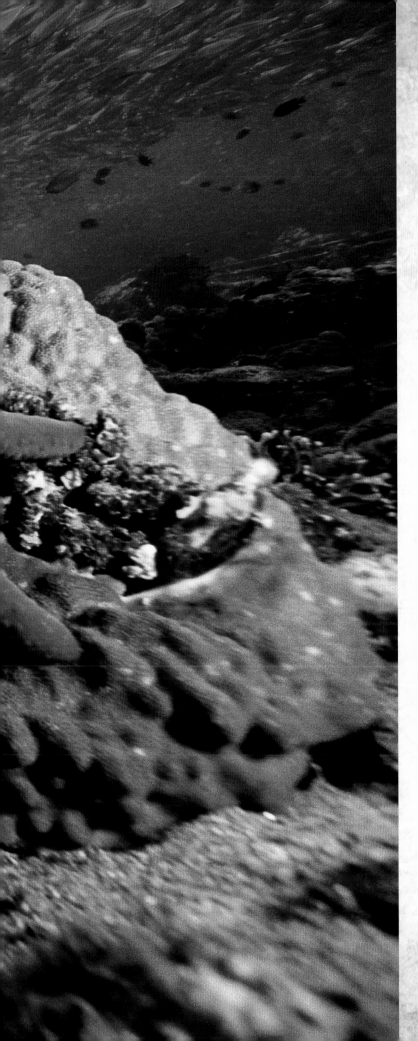

Until I Saw the Sea

Until I saw the sea
I did not know
that wind
could wrinkle water so.

I never knew
that sun
could splinter a whole sea of blue.

Nor
did I know before,
a sea breathes in and out
upon a shore.

—Lilian Moore

What Are Heavy?

What are heavy? Sea-sand and sorrow:
What are brief? To-day and to-morrow:
What are frail? Spring blossoms and youth:
What are deep? The ocean and truth.

—*Christina Rossetti*

The Dead Sea

*A salt lake bordering Jordan to the east
and Israel and Palestine to the west*

Somewhere down and down below
at the bottom of the bottom, this place
claims no skeletons or bones
under its brackish face;

it spits a rain of brimstone
in a sulphur somersault,
from out of the dark it bubbles
with salt
          and salt
                  and salt.

—Rebecca Kai Dotlich

SALT CRYSTALS, DEAD SEA, ISRAEL

Like Ghosts of Eagles

The Indians have mostly gone
but not before they named the rivers
the rivers flow on
and the names of the rivers flow with them
  Susquehanna   Shenandoah

The rivers are now polluted plundered
but not the names of the rivers
cool and inviolate as ever
pure as on the morning of creation
  Tennessee   Tombigbee

If the rivers themselves should ever perish
I think the names will somehow somewhere hover
like ghosts of eagles
those mighty whisperers
  Missouri   Mississippi.

—Robert Francis

BLUE SPRING, MISSOURI, U.S.A.

Ammonites: Sculptures of the Sea

Nestled in the outermost chamber
of their self-sculpted spirals,
ammonites sleep deep till nightfall,

safely ascend to the ocean surface—
letting air into each chamber—
then scavenge till daylight

signals them to silently sink
back down on their sides
like rugged handmade plates.

—Betsy Franco

AMMONITE SPIRAL SNAIL FOSSIL

53

Where Go the Boats?

Dark brown is the river,
Golden is the sand.
It flows along for ever,
With trees on either hand.

Green leaves a-floating,
Castles of the foam,
Boats of mine a-boating—
Where will all come home?

On goes the river
And out past the mill,
Away down the valley,
Away down the hill.

Away down the river,
A hundred miles or more,
Other little children
Shall bring my boats ashore.

—*Robert Louis Stevenson*

The Mill Back Home

Logs drowse in the pond
Dreaming of their heroes
Alligator and crocodile

—*Vern Rutsala*

ROCK CREEK, WASHINGTON, D.C., U.S.A.

BAYOU SAUVAGE NATIONAL WILDLIFE REFUGE, LOUISIANA, U.S.A.

In the Salt Marsh

How faithfully grass holds the shape of the sea it loves,
how it molds itself to the waves, how the dried salt
peaks into cowlicks the combed mane of the marsh.
Tousled by tides, it pitches tents, breaks into turrets
and coxcombs and whorled nests and green baskets
for the bleached armor of fiddler crabs, like earrings
hung by the sea on lobes of darkness. Could I lay my ear
on that darkness where the tide's trowel smooths islands
and scallops the sand, moon-tugged, till it slows
and turns? Could I keep the past in the present's eye?
Could I know what the grass knows?

—*Nancy Willard*

Take Bus **9** to the **Red Sea Beach**

and come prepared. An endless flat
grows nothing green or natural,
but a weed rolls out the Welcome Mat,
red as your blood, to the unwell.

Here things catch things. Cranes stab
the mud for clam or crab,
the river looping aimlessly
cannot find the sea,
and warnings posted up ahead
are in language that cannot be read.

Out on the Bay they drill for oil.
The towers rise as if to say
"Pollution can be beautiful.
That is the lesson for today."

—*John Barr*

SCULPTURE OF RED-CROWNED CRANE, RED SEA BEACH, CHINA

CHRISTMAS ISLAND RED CRABS, CHRISTMAS ISLAND, AUSTRALIA

The Red Crabs of Christmas Island

From the forest, males are sprawling.
Over craggy cliffs, they're crawling,
scuttling toward the sea.

Into sandy shores, they furrow,
digging a protective burrow,
near the sounding sea.

Now the frantic females hurry.
To the waiting males they scurry,
skittering toward the sea.

Eggs are laid where water's creeping.
Waves come closer, sweeping, sweeping
egg sacs out to sea.

Baby crabs, born in the ocean,
synchronize their sideways motion.
Millions leave the seas,

and head back to the trees.

—B. J. Lee

The
Great
BLUE HOLE

Off the coast of Belize

Dark, dead, no current
four hundred feet deep

Rise now from the bottom, peer into
an ancient, gaping cavern as you ascend, touch
stalactites hanging like monstrous jungle vines, meet
sleek reef sharks circling, shadows in shallows, feel
the reassuring slope of sandy limestone shelf, spot
sunlit coral fringe, turtles, tropical fish, and

Break through! Breathe air! Surface
into the last ice age, witness
water carve cave from rock, gasp
as the sea rushes in, tremble
as a dry roof collapses, flee
as formation drowns, marvel

as it is sucked into vast chasm
abyss of blue intensity born

—*Donna Marie Merritt*

I Owe It All to Water

The Great Blue Hole, Belize

Back in the ice age,
I became a cave.
In my hollow heart, I meditated
on my maker.

Water's three little atoms have such power:
dripping steadily,
grinding microscopically,
sculpting artistically.

Suddenly
(or so it seemed)
the oceans rose, my ceiling fell, and I was completely
submerged. Filled to the brim. Literally.

Now I am a deep, indigo blue. A circular
sapphire in a turquoise sea: singular.
Breathtakingly spectacular.
And I owe it all to water.

—*Mary Lee Hahn*

HOLTUN CENOTE, MEXICO

ON THE

MOVE

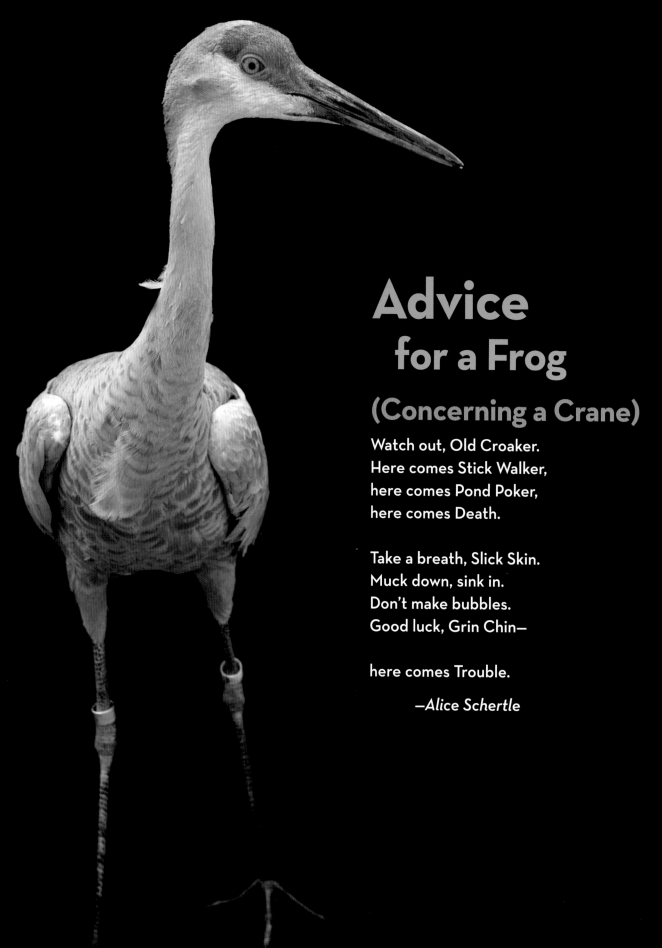

Advice
for a Frog
(Concerning a Crane)

Watch out, Old Croaker.
Here comes Stick Walker,
here comes Pond Poker,
here comes Death.

Take a breath, Slick Skin.
Muck down, sink in.
Don't make bubbles.
Good luck, Grin Chin—

here comes Trouble.

—Alice Schertle

FLORIDA SANDHILL CRANE

The Clown Fish

Is not an enemy
of anemone;
in fact, it is anemone's maid,
for which anemone
stings its enemies.
And that's how friends are made.

—*David Elliott*

CLOWNFISH AND ANEMONE

A Blessing

Just off the highway to Rochester, Minnesota,
Twilight bounds softly forth on the grass.
And the eyes of those two Indian ponies
Darken with kindness.
They have come gladly out of the willows
To welcome my friend and me.
We step over the barbed wire into the pasture
Where they have been grazing all day, alone.
They ripple tensely, they can hardly contain their happiness
That we have come.
They bow shyly as wet swans. They love each other.
There is no loneliness like theirs.
At home once more,
They begin munching the young tufts of spring in the darkness.
I would like to hold the slenderer one in my arms,
For she has walked over to me
And nuzzled my left hand.
She is black and white,
Her mane falls wild on her forehead,
And the light breeze moves me to caress her long ear
That is delicate as the skin over a girl's wrist.
Suddenly I realize
That if I stepped out of my body I would break
Into blossom.

—James Wright

ICELANDIC HORSES

The Rhea

The rhea rheally isn't strange—
It's just an ostrich, rhearranged.

—*Douglas Florian*

Queen Alexandra's Birdwing

This largest and loveliest, last of its kind,
is the jewel of the jungle. Its wings unveil
iridescence that flies off the radiance scale.
Emerald and sapphire so finely designed!
Butterfly rarest and hardest to find.

—*Avis Harley*

QUEEN ALEXANDRA'S BIRDWING BUTTERFLY

Everything Old Becomes New

Everything old becomes new before it dies.
Chrysalis, a moment before the butterflies
stretch those limp and limpid wings,
makes a sound, almost sings,
exchanges breath with its quaking new life.
Egg about to crack before the beak's sure knife
remembers warmth inside the hen.
Mountain crumbles into its own ravine.

And you walking the Devon hills
remark the old year, watching the spills
of winter sun blaze the ancient landscape there
before the turning of the fading year.
Everything old, dear friend, anew.
Even me, even you.

—*Jane Yolen*

Gym on a Rock

I watch a lizard
doing push-ups in the sun—
a tiny buff man.

—Sonya Sones

FOREST CRESTED LIZARD

Electric Eel

Some think Electric Eel lacks looks,
But others find it stunning.
A homegrown battery it packs
To keep its shocker running.

Why, you could light all New York's streets
And skyscrapers and stuff
With one Electric Eel alone
If it were long enough.

—X. J. Kennedy

ELECTRIC EEL

On the Grasshopper and Cricket

The poetry of earth is never dead:
    When all the birds are faint with the hot sun,
    And hide in cooling trees, a voice will run
From hedge to hedge about the new-mown mead;
That is the Grasshopper's—he takes the lead
    In summer luxury,—he has never done
    With his delights; for when tired out with fun
He rests at ease beneath some pleasant weed.
The poetry of earth is ceasing never:
    On a lone winter evening, when the frost
    Has wrought a silence, from the stove there shrills
The Cricket's song, in warmth increasing ever,
    And seems to one in drowsiness half lost,
    The Grasshopper's among some grassy hills.

                —*John Keats*

The Flower-Fed Buffaloes

The flower-fed buffaloes of the spring
In the days of long ago,
Ranged where the locomotives sing
And the prairie flowers lie low:—
The tossing, blooming, perfumed grass
Is swept away by the wheat,
Wheels and wheels and wheels spin by
In the spring that still is sweet.
But the flower-fed buffaloes of the spring
Left us, long ago.
They gore no more, they bellow no more,
They trundle around the hills no more:—
With the Blackfeet, lying low,
With the Pawnees, lying low,
Lying low.

—Vachel Lindsay

BUFFALO, GRAND TETON NATIONAL PARK, WYOMING, U.S.A.

The Difference Between Frog and Toad

The look-alike of *frog* is *toad*;
They have a similar dress code.
A *frog* has skin that's smooth and slimy;
A *toad*'s complexion's warty and dry;
A *frog* would like to kiss a princess;
A *toad* prefers to kiss a fly.

—*Anonymous*

RED-EYED TREE FROG

BALD EAGLE

The Ways of Living Things

There is wonder past all wonder
in the ways of living things,
in a worm's intrepid wriggling,
in the song a blackbird sings,

In the grandeur of an eagle
and the fury of a shark,
in the calmness of a tortoise
on a meadow in the dark,

In the splendor of a sea gull
as it plummets from the sky,
in the incandescent shimmer
of a noisy dragonfly,

In a heron, still and silent
underneath a crescent moon,
in a butterfly emerging
from its silver-spun cocoon.

In a fish's joyful splashing,
in a snake that makes no sound,
in the smallest salamander
there is wonder to be found.

—Jack Prelutsky

Quail's Nest

I wandered out one rainy day
    And heard a bird with merry joys
Cry "wet my foot" for half the way;
    I stood and wondered at the noise,

When from my foot a bird did flee—
    The rain flew bouncing from her breast
I wondered what the bird could be,
    And almost trampled on her nest.

The nest was full of eggs and round—
    I met a shepherd in the vales,
And stood to tell him what I found.
    He knew and said it was a quail's,

For he himself the nest had found,
    Among the wheat and on the green,
When going on his daily round,
    With eggs as many as fifteen.

Among the stranger birds they feed,
    Their summer flight is short and low;
There's very few know where they breed,
    And scarcely anywhere they go.

                    —John Clare

QUAIL EGGS IN NEST

Cardinal Nest

Tiptoe up and look real closely
made with sticks and straw but mostly
made with love and lots of care
a little tree house in the air.

—*Charles Ghigna*

Self-Pity

I never saw a wild thing
sorry for itself.
A small bird will drop frozen dead from a bough
without ever having felt sorry for itself.

—*D. H. Lawrence*

WHALE

A whale is stout about the middle,
He is stout about the ends,
& so is all his family
& so are all his friends.

He's pleased that he's enormous,
He's happy he weighs tons,
& so are all his daughters
& so are all his sons.

He eats when he is hungry
Each kind of food he wants,
& so do all his uncles
& so do all his aunts.

He doesn't mind his blubber,
He doesn't mind his creases,
& neither do his nephews
& neither do his nieces.

You may find him chubby,
You may find him fat,
But he would disagree with you:
He likes himself like that.

—Mary Ann Hoberman

Sips
of
Sea

the
pipe
fish
seems
to
me
to
be
a
straw
to
draw
up
sips
of
sea

—Avis Harley

GULF PIPEFISH

The Answers

"When did the world begin and how?"
I asked a lamb, a goat, a cow:

"What's it all about and why?"
I asked a hog as he went by:

"Where will the whole thing end, and when?"
I asked a duck, a goose, a hen:

And I copied all the answers too,
A quack, a honk, an oink, a moo.

—*Robert Clairmont*

Advice from the Scorpion

Do not be afraid, *amigo*.
Walk softly through the silent crowd
Of cactus men and cholla boys—
The touch-me-nots of the desert.
Here in scrub country,
I am a touch-me-not too—
The Land Lobster, sideways-dancing.

Do not be afraid, *amiga*.
The screaming you hear
Is only the yellow-breasted chat
Scolding the purple-mad sky.
Even in the Land of Little Rain,
Five-legged Lightning
Can break Moon's heart.

—*J. Patrick Lewis*

Centipede

Beneath the lawn, on the slimy bottoms
of logs and stones,
among the fallen, rotten, and sodden,
where every root
hoards the alchemy of sunbeams,
the centipedes
create the planet's future, turning
what once had been
into what yet might be: an aspen,
a milkweed pod,
a pumpkin, or a field of beans.

—*Michael J. Rosen*

The BOA

Just when you think you know the boa,
There's moa and moa and moa and moa.

—*Douglas Florian*

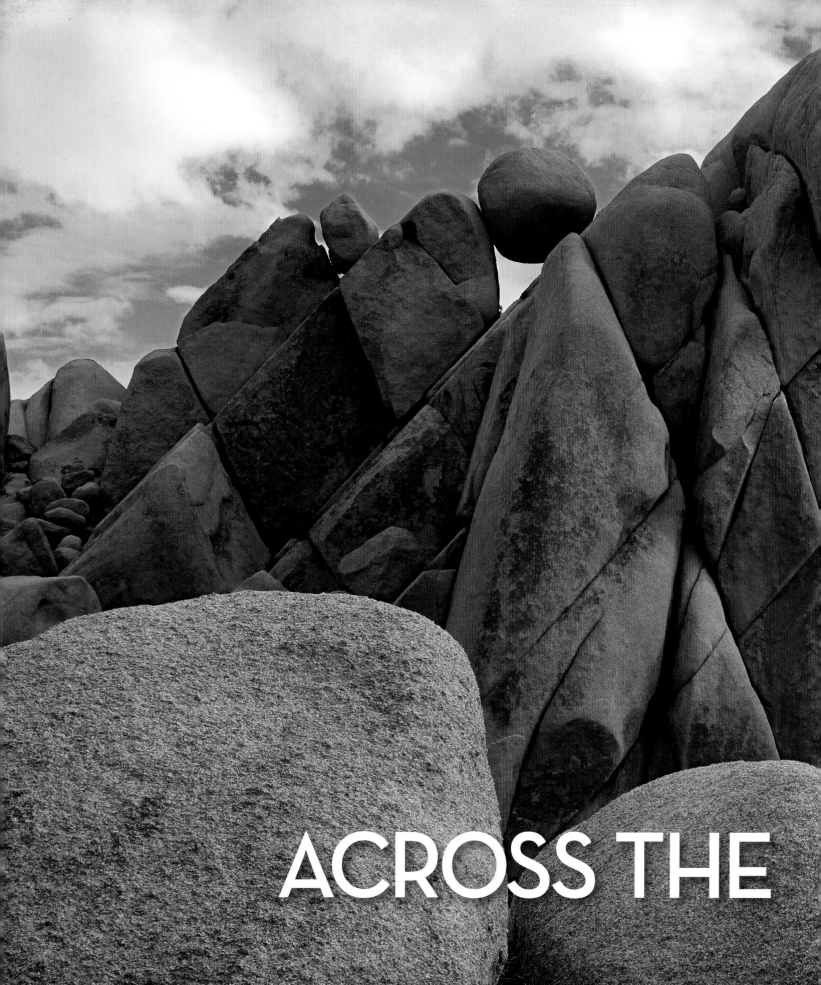

ACROSS THE

JOSHUA TREE NATIONAL PARK, CALIFORNIA, U.S.A.

LAND

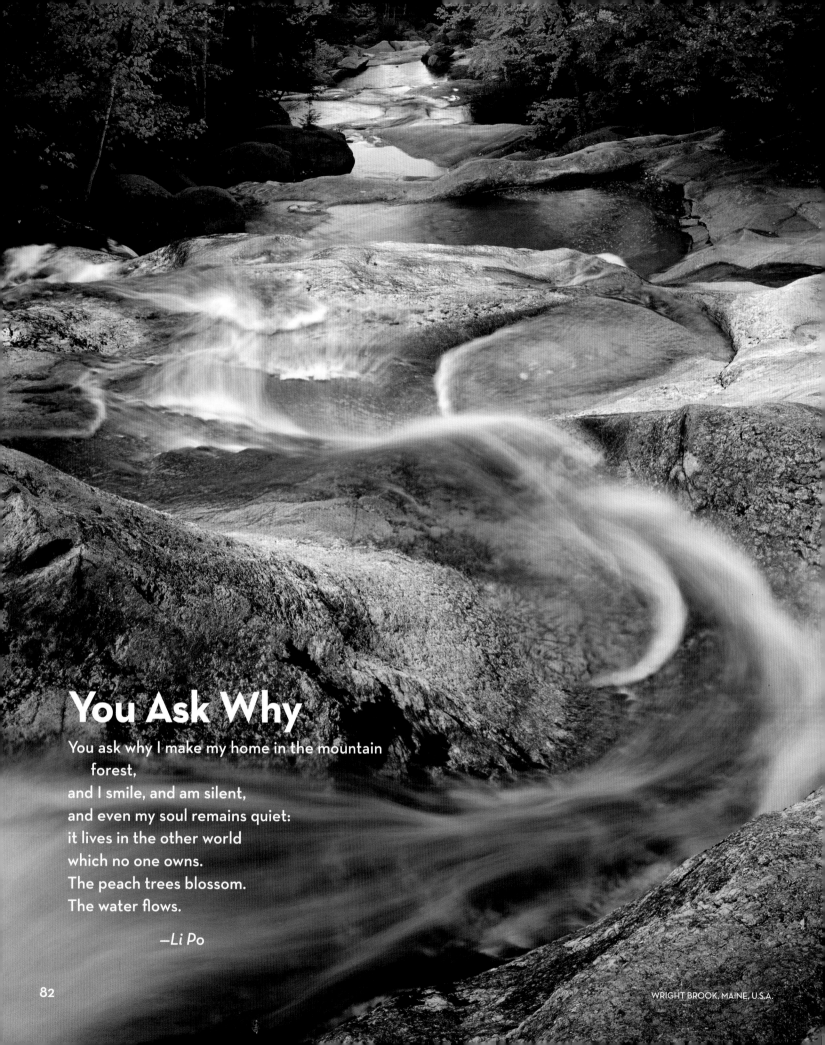

You Ask Why

You ask why I make my home in the mountain
    forest,
and I smile, and am silent,
and even my soul remains quiet:
it lives in the other world
which no one owns.
The peach trees blossom.
The water flows.

—*Li Po*

WRIGHT BROOK, MAINE, U.S.A.

across the land

To Make
a Prairie

To make a prairie it takes a clover and one bee,
One clover, and a bee,
And revery.
The revery alone will do
If bees are few.

—Emily Dickinson

An Indian
Summer Day
on the Prairie

(IN THE BEGINNING)
The sun is a huntress young,
The sun is a red, red joy,
The sun is an Indian girl,
Of the tribe of the Illinois.

(MID-MORNING)
The sun is a smouldering fire,
That creeps through the high gray plain,
And leaves not a bush of cloud
To blossom with flowers of rain.

(NOON)
The sun is a wounded deer,
That treads pale grass in the skies,
Shaking his golden horns,
Flashing his baleful eyes.

(SUNSET)
The sun is an eagle old,
There in the windless west.
Atop of the spirit-cliffs
He builds him a crimson nest.

—Vachel Lindsay

Afternoon on a Hill

I will be the gladdest thing
Under the sun!
I will touch a hundred flowers
And not pick one.

I will look at cliffs and clouds
With quiet eyes,
Watch the wind bow down the grass,
And the grass rise.

And when lights begin to show
Up from the town,
I will mark which must be mine,
And then start down!

—*Edna St. Vincent Millay*

Up on the Hill

I have been up on the side of the hill
And looked at the world till I looked my fill.

I walked and watched two distant showers,
Then sat and dreamed the hill was ours.

How does it feel to be on high?
Full as you hope to feel when you die.

—*James Hayford*

Adlestrop

Yes. I remember Adlestrop—
The name, because one afternoon
Of heat the express-train drew up there
Unwontedly. It was late June.

The steam hissed. Someone cleared his
        throat.
No one left and no one came
On the bare platform. What I saw
Was Adlestrop—only the name

And willows, willow-herb, and grass,
And meadowsweet, and haycocks dry,
No whit less still and lonely fair
Than the high cloudlets in the sky.

And for that minute a blackbird sang
Close by, and round him, mistier,
Farther and farther, all the birds
Of Oxfordshire and Gloucestershire.

—*Edward Thomas*

POPPIES AND WILDFLOWERS, CALIFORNIA, U.S.A.

from Bat Cave

The cave looked much like any other
from a little distance but
as we approached, came almost
to its mouth, we saw its walls within
that slanted up into a dome
were beating like a wild black lung—
it was plastered and hung with
the pulsing bodies of bats, the organ
music of the body's deep
interior, alive, the sacred cave
with its ten thousand gleaming eyes
near the clustered rocks
where the sea beat with the leather
wings of its own dark waves.

—*Eleanor Wilner*

MEXICAN FREE-TAILED BATS

BEAVERTAIL CACTUS, CALIFORNIA, U.S.A.

Desert

I want to be there when the desert blooms
To see hot pink and shining gold
    interrupt the endless tan
To dance among the cactuses
    sporting flowers in their spiky hair
To celebrate the birth of tadpoles
    swimming in sudden pools

I want to be there when the desert blooms
To watch this serious span of earth
    grow festive for a day
To revel in rain as something
    sacred and rare
To honor this peculiar place
    where hope is not for fools

—Marilyn Singer

At the Un-National Monument Along the Canadian Border

This is the field where the battle did not happen,
where the unknown soldier did not die.
This is the field where grass joined hands,
where no monument stands,
and the only heroic thing is the sky.

Birds fly here without any sound,
unfolding their wings across the open.
No people killed—or were killed—on this ground
hallowed by neglect and an air so tame
that people celebrate it by forgetting its name.

—William Stafford

Former Barn Lot

Once there was a fence here,
    And the grass came and tried,
Leaning from the pasture,
    To get inside.

But colt feet trampled it,
    Turning it brown;
Until the farmer moved
    And the fence fell down.

Then any bird saw,
    Under the wire,
Grass nibbling inward
    Like green fire.

—Mark Van Doren

Red Rides West

Red buries green—*Autumn.*

*

Red marries yellow—*Sunset.*

*

Red rides west—*Sundown.*

*

Red hides soil—*Dust.*

*

Red burns orange—*Embers.*

*

Red turns gray—*Ashes.*

*

Red goes gold—*Evening.*

*

Red grows old—*Rust.*

—*Mariel Bede*

ARCHES NATIONAL PARK, UTAH, U.S.A.

Sailing Stone

Observed at Racetrack Playa,
Death Valley National Park, California, U.S.A.
and elsewhere

This immovable stone leaves a smooth, stunning trail
in Death Valley's vastness—distinctly alone.
But behind it, a path of reverse rocky braille—
this *immovable* stone?

How it moved is the question; the answer's unknown.
How does a boulder go for a sail?
Nobody dragged it—it didn't get thrown.

Was it blown by December's fast, frosty exhale?
Did it move by some magical force of its own?
Science hides truth behind mystery's veil:
this immovable stone.

—Laura Purdie Salas

In a **Quiet Dark Place**

The first drop leaves calcium—
a minuscule ring—
more molecules on the floor.

Drop by drop
fragile forms begin, stretch
down
up
an inch every 200 years.

Unknowable time,
from different places
moist tips draw near.

The moment comes,
inevitable union,
destiny sealed.

First touch in the dark,
gentle as a lover's kiss,
join them at last as one.

—*David L. Harrison*

ONONDAGA CAVE, MISSOURI, U.S.A.

Thank You Note to the Gorge

At Watkins Glen State Park,
New York, U.S.A.

Gorge,

You are like a Chinese brush painting,
all lichened rocks and crags,
jutting precipices, scraggly pines.
As tourists passed, I stood
and stared at a waterfall that tumbled
down your rocks in a spray of joy.

Halfway up your narrow stone path
I was out of breath. I stopped to watch
waters of yet another fall slide over you—
a transparent skin
that crashed in foamy froth.

Your cold air, deep shadows,
endless stone steps,
all shrouded in a strange green daytime light
made a mystery around me, and I felt
as though I were in some far and ancient land.

Thank you, gorge, for the wonder of my trip.

—Patricia Hubbell

WATKINS GLEN GORGE, NEW YORK, U.S.A.

ROADS IN AUTUMN

A Late Walk

When I go up through the mowing field,
The headless aftermath,
Smooth-laid like thatch with the heavy dew,
Half closes the garden path.

And when I come to the garden ground,
The whir of sober birds
Up from the tangle of withered weeds
Is sadder than any words.

A tree beside the wall stands bare,
But a leaf that lingered brown,
Disturbed, I doubt not, by my thought,
Comes softly rattling down.

I end not far from my going forth
By picking the faded blue
Of the last remaining aster flower
To carry again to you.

—*Robert Frost*

The Song of Wandering Aengus

I went out to the hazel wood,
Because a fire was in my head,
And cut and peeled a hazel wand,
And hooked a berry to a thread;
And when white moths were on the wing,
And moth-like stars were flickering out,
I dropped the berry in a stream
And caught a little silver trout.

When I had laid it on the floor
I went to blow the fire a-flame,
But something rustled on the floor,
And someone called me by my name:
It had become a glimmering girl
With apple blossom in her hair
Who called me by my name and ran
And faded through the brightening air.

Though I am old with wandering
Through hollow lands and hilly lands,
I will find out where she has gone,
And kiss her lips and take her hands;
And walk among long dappled grass,
And pluck till time and times are done,
The silver apples of the moon,
The golden apples of the sun.

—*William Butler Yeats*

Nature's Calm

The mountain brows, the rocks, the peaks, are sleeping,
Uplands and gorges hush!
The thousand moorland things are stillness keeping;
The beasts under each bush
Crouch, and the hivèd bees
Rest in their honeyed ease;
In the purple sea fish lie as they were dead,
And each bird folds his wing over his head.

—Alcman

Translated by Edwin Arnold

The Mountains— Grow Unnoticed

The Mountains—grow unnoticed —
Their Purple figures rise
Without attempt—Exhaustion—
Assistance—or Applause—

In Their Eternal Faces
The Sun—with just delight
Looks long—and last—and golden—
For Fellowship—at night—

—Emily Dickinson

A LONE TREE, VENDÉE, FRANCE

IN
SHADE

Lessons in September

In the first golden hour of autumn
when light slants away from summer's angry eye
and the leaves, not yet blushing, mute and soften
I went to the woods
with nothing to tether me to this world—
to remember how to listen
to the wind cascade through leaves in cresting waves
to finches squabble like tetchy spouses
to the soft music of the creek.
To remember how to see
a spotted toad vault into the underbrush
a white caterpillar wend its way across the footbridge
a red-tailed hawk slide past the window of sky.
A birch tree, I've passed hundreds of times
without notice, stood sentinel all the same.
Someday, I hope to stay
who I am in the woods
when out of them—
Aware
Grateful
Awed

—*Tracie Vaughn Zimmer*

Time to Plant Trees

Time to plant trees is when you're young
So you will have them to walk among—

So, aging, you can walk in shade
That you and time together made.

—*James Hayford*

Dew

Diamonds on the petals,
Silver on the stems,
Early morning sunrise
Turns dewdrops into gems.

—*Charles Ghigna*

BLUEBELLS

Butterfly Tree

Like some
Hawaiian king
draped in a feathered robe,
eucalyptus reigns—resplendent
monarch.

—*Joan Bransfield Graham*

MONARCH BUTTERFLIES, SIERRA CHINCUA, MEXICO

The Monarch's Flight to Mexico

Only a whisper from ancient roots
and cyclones of orange rise.
Good-bye to summer's sweet pursuits!
Only a whisper from ancient roots,
and billions dressed in brilliant suits
ride skyways billed for butterflies.
Only a whisper from ancient roots,
and cyclones of orange rise.

—*Avis Harley*

101

Haiku

lily:
out of the water . . .
out of itself

—*Nick Virgilio*

EGYPTIAN BLUE WATER LILY

General Sherman Sequoia: World's Largest Tree

Giant Forest of Sequoia National Park, Tulare County, California, U.S.A.

General Sherman,
though elements
batter you—wind,
fire . . . storms—
you deflect them,
hold your ground.
For 2,500 years
you have watched
the rise and fall of
lives, civilizations.
At 275' tall, you
have captured a
corner of the sky.
Stand victorious:
we s a l u t e you.

—*Joan Bransfield Graham*

Sequoia

In the very middle
of the archaic woods
leaves browse on the sun
like gods, roots tongue
the dark below—who
needs words? I find
myself debating silence,
losing again.

—*Leonard Nathan*

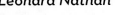
GENERAL SHERMAN TREE, SEQUOIA NATIONAL PARK, CALIFORNIA, U.S.A.

The Mystery

The tree is the mystery,
its roots knotted
as surely as love.

The spring flowers are the mystery,
without calendar or clock
they announce the season.

The pond is the mystery,
holding trout in its deepest,
darkest heart.

The fern is the mystery,
knowing how to uncurl
with no teacher but the sun.

The path is the mystery,
worn down by many feet
yet still willing to support them.

The gate . . .
    the gate is no mystery at all
for we have put it there
to signal that house is near,

though dog has but to lift his snout
to know we are already home.

—*Jane Yolen*

in shade

Bouquets

One flower at a time, please
however small the face.

Two flowers are one flower
too many, a distraction.

Three flowers in a vase begin
to be a little noisy

Like cocktail conversation,
everybody talking.

A crowd of flowers is a crowd
of flatterers (forgive me).

One flower at a time. I want
to hear what it is saying.

—*Robert Francis*

RED POPPY

Beside a Chrysanthemum

For one chrysanthemum to bloom
a nightingale
has sobbed since spring, perhaps.

For one chrysanthemum to bloom
thunder
has pealed in dark clouds, perhaps.

Flower! Like my sister standing
at her mirror, just back
from far away, far away byways of youth,
where she was racked with longing and lack:

last night's frost came down
to bid your yellow petals bloom, perhaps,
while I could not get to sleep.

—So Chong Ju

Translated by Brother Anthony of Taize

BUTTON CHRYSANTHEMUMS   WHITE BIRCHES, COLORADO, U.S.A.

Counting-Out Rhyme

Silver bark of beech, and sallow
Bark of yellow birch and yellow
   Twig of willow.

Stripe of green in moosewood maple,
Colour seen in leaf of apple,
   Bark of popple.

Wood of popple pale as moonbeam,
Wood of oak for yoke and barn-beam,
   Wood of hornbeam.

Silver bark of beech, and hollow
Stem of elder, tall and yellow
   Twig of willow.

—*Edna St. Vincent Millay*

The **Release**

At sunset
the shadows of all the trees
break free and go running
across the edge of the world.

—*Joseph Bruchac*

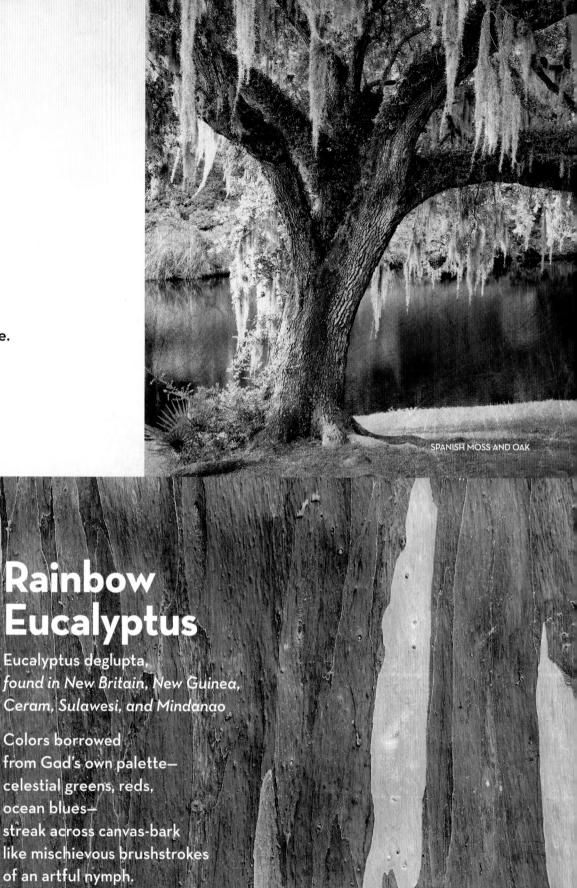

Spanish Moss

A Southern Gothic,
A Live Oak lady,
Caressing limbs,
Secret and shady.

Wild and pale,
Curly and thin,
She's a tease in the breeze.
She sways in the wind.

—Charles Ghigna

SPANISH MOSS AND OAK

Rainbow Eucalyptus

Eucalyptus deglupta,
*found in New Britain, New Guinea,
Ceram, Sulawesi, and Mindanao*

Colors borrowed
from God's own palette—
celestial greens, reds,
ocean blues—
streak across canvas-bark
like mischievous brushstrokes
of an artful nymph.

—Matt Forrest Esenwine

RAINBOW EUCALYPTUS BARK

Blow-up

Our cherry tree
Unfolds whole loads
Of pink-white blooms—
It just explodes.

For three short days
Its petals last.
Oh, what a waste.
But what a blast.

—*X. J. Kennedy*

CHERRY BLOSSOM

Bougainvillea

Tissue blossoms
bright as lips
start drifting with the breeze,

looping low and
twirling up
in between the trees,

a swath of color,
drooping slowly,
falling down to lie

on the ground.
Watch out! Don't step
on that pink butterfly.

—*Ann Whitford Paul*

PINK BOUGAINVILLEA

109

How to Bake a Flower

Stir seeds into well-drained soil.
Fold in a half-cup live worms.

Sprinkle in occasional rain
until green shoots appear.

Blend in sun mixed with shade.
Add a dash of moonlight.

Simmer on low four to six weeks
in the unhurried oven of summer.

When the air starts smelling sweet
it's ready to be served—almost.

Swirl in butterflies.
Whip in bees.

—Ralph Fletcher

BEE ON COSMOS

TOADSTOOLS ON RAIN FOREST FLOOR, ECUADOR

Mushroom Hunting

Two girls bent in the wet woods wondering
why the heavenly mushrooms withered.
One said we have come at the wrong time
of year. One said nothing.

The one who said nothing said nothing
comes here.

A congress of clouds met just above:
The timothy bowed, the larkspur shied.
Miles away, a fox formed into a fox.

And the one who said nothing said nothing
comes here.

—*Peter Kostin*

Milkweeds, November

Now the brown and withered pods all break
into wide-mouthed grins. Each seed escapes
with a tuft of white for its body—if "body" can be
lighter than the waft of a monarch's lifting wing.

After the briefest flight, the seed heads drop
like the empty parachutes of dreams,
releasing—we called them "fairies" (finding no word
for what seemed equal parts wing and web

and wayward star from the Milky Way)—to float
across the asphalt and grass and into our rooms:
each an asterisk of air, a wish
the milkweed sent with hope's whispered breath.

Oh, to catch one
in a swat of your hand!

—*Michael J. Rosen*

COMMON MILKWEED

DAFFODILS

in shade

I Wandered Lonely as a Cloud

I wandered lonely as a cloud
That floats on high o'er vales and hills,
When all at once I saw a crowd,
A host, of golden daffodils;
Beside the lake, beneath the trees,
Fluttering and dancing in the breeze.

Continuous as the stars that shine
And twinkle on the milky way,
They stretched in never-ending line
Along the margin of a bay:
Ten thousand saw I at a glance,
Tossing their heads in sprightly dance.

The waves beside them danced; but they
Out-did the sparkling waves in glee:
A poet could not but be gay,
In such a jocund company:
I gazed—and gazed—but little thought
What wealth the show to me had brought:

For oft, when on my couch I lie
In vacant or in pensive mood,
They flash upon that inward eye
Which is the bliss of solitude;
And then my heart with pleasure fills,
And dances with the daffodils.

—William Wordsworth

The Methuselah Tree: Ancient Bristlecone Pine Forest

Inyo County, eastern California, U.S.A.

Up here
on the slopes
of the White Mountains,
there is silence,
as if the world
is holding its breath.
When I was young,
pyramids rose
from the sands
of Egypt. Now,
almost 5,000 years old,
I am called
"living driftwood,"
awash in a sea of time,
sinew against sky
against century, I
am the oldest
living thing
on
earth.

—Joan Bransfield Graham

METHUSELAH, A GREAT BASIN BRISTLECONE PINE, CALIFORNIA, U.S.A.

Rose

The story goes:
don't stick your nose
inside a rose
because of bees.
But knees,
bare toes,
and—ouch!—
elbows
are the parts
the prickles
hurt the most
when a ball gets thrown
in an overgrown bush
and you need to—
ouch!—
just reach an inch.
No one warns you:
roses pinch!

—*Janet S. Wong*

Mirrorment

Birds are flowers flying
and flowers perched birds.

—A. R. Ammons

Pine Tree in January

A cone of green against stark white
Through wind and snow upright it stands,
Prickle point needle fingered hands
Spike sharp into the winter's night.
Remaining leaved once Autumn's been
Implies bristled tenacity.
Outwardly, an unfriendly tree,
Yet cardinals nestle warm within.

—Michael Salinger

IN
DIST

HURRICANE IGOR AS SEEN FROM SPACE

RESS

Avalanche

Hardpack buckles
Up from below.
Bare white knuckles

Jut through snow.
A yeti's paw
Begins to grow

Claw by claw.
And mountainside,
Softened by thaw,

Unearths a tide
For fractured slabs
Of snow to ride.

The monster grabs
At all in its path,
Heaves and jabs

With wintry wrath
Aspens bowed
In aftermath,

Leaving a shroud
Of powder cloud!

—*Steven Withrow*

AVALANCHE, PARADISE BAY, ANTARCTICA

Dormant Dragons

Volcanoes there are that sleep
    the sleep of dragons
with cool heads and hot bellies
    they crouch
        solid and still
    where the earth meets the sky
Till something wakes them
      Then furious they breathe fire and smoke
          hot spittle and wrath
    to burn and choke
        whatever lies in their path
leaving in their wake
      an odd treasure
of stone sponges and glass
      and an occasional lake

—Marilyn Singer

MOUNT ETNA, SICILY, ITALY

Tsunami

Five hundred miles per hour, the core
sweeps under every ship to shore,
unleashing megatons of sea-
floor-detonating energy

to flatten village, field, and road—
Mother Nature's mother lode—
at unsuspecting ports of call.
An ocean-blown Niagara fall.

—Anonymous

Weather Deniers

How can you deny the change
when January has become
the very Florida of the year?
Thermometers perspire,
inspire walkers, who stride
across missing snowbanks,
arms bare.

   Are you unaware
that this is no ordinary thaw?
There's a flaw in your thinking.
Mud and bud before March.
Even the daffodils are threatening,
raising their green shafts
like swords, and squirrels
digging up their buried nuts.

       —Jane Yolen

Tsunami

The wave travels silently
without companions,
gathering them into itself.

Passing through
everything
like a ghost,

it rushes with something
to tell the shore.
But by the time it arrives

it can only roar.

       —JonArno Lawson

TSUNAMI, FUKUSHIMA PREFECTURE, JAPAN

Earthquake

Dakota, first to sense a change,
Begins to whimper—passing strange.

Here comes the catastrophic whine:
The loss is yours, the fault is mine.

Tectonic plates can only shake
A continental bellyache

By stretching several feet or more
To rearrange themselves before

The settlements of Earth lie bare
Among the rubble of despair.

—*Mariel Bede*

LAVIC LAKE FAULT, CALIFORNIA, U.S.A.

Fire **and Ice**

Some say the world will end in fire,
Some say in ice.
From what I've tasted of desire
I hold with those who favor fire.
But if it had to perish twice,
I think I know enough of hate
To say that for destruction ice
Is also great
And would suffice.

—*Robert Frost*

Drought

Interminable
    Dynamo,
This dry disaster
    Takes it slow.

A random rain,
    Long promised, stops
The riverbeds
    And withers crops.

For those without
    A water source,
The famine runs
    Its tragic course:

First thirst, then fever,
    Endless sun . . .
The waiting for
    Oblivion.

      —Peter Kostin

SOSSUSVLEI, NAMIBIA

TORNADO SEASON

Wind went by with people falling out of it,
and hairpins,
and a barn door swinging without its hinges.
Grass rose in swarms along with nails.
A crow flew upside down,
his legs reaching skyward,
and growing longer.

—Adrien Stoutenburg

TORNADO, COLORADO, U.S.A.

Punishing Conditions

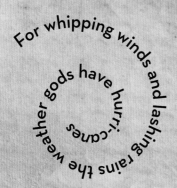

For whipping winds and lashing rains the weather gods have hurri-canes.

—Graham Denton

Where Will We Run To

Where will we run to
when the moon's
polluted in its turn

and the sun sits
with its wheels blocked
in the used
       star
          lot?

—X. J. Kennedy

The Merry-Go-Round Song

What shall we do with the ozone layer?
What shall we do, Daddy dear?
We'll knit the clouds into tight white shrouds
And stitch them with needles of fear.

The clock is striking, oh is it too late?
Have we run out of time, Mummy dear?
With our ladder of cars, we shall climb to the stars
To create a new atmosphere.

But when will we learn the lesson we must?
When will we learn, Brother dear?
We will learn how to fly like a plane in the sky
What a gas! (that won't disappear).

And is the earth leaking and what of her wounds?
Oh what of her wounds, Sister dear?
To plug up the hole, we shall fill it with coal
Though it bleeds with a dark oily smear.

What shall we do with the ozone layer?
Don't worry your head, my dear.
Now hide your tears and close up your ears
For nobody wants to hear.

—Andrew Fusek Peters and Polly Peters

 *in distress*

Birds Have Left
Without a Song

Birds have left without a song.
Morning light looks yellow and wrong.
Airports close, so does the town.
Winds pick up, trees blow down.
Radios go on and on.
Churches fill, church bells bong.
The people are listening, listening.

Born in a land Saharas away
Crossing an ocean to have its say
Crashing through town like a runaway train
Oh Breaker of Nations rain us your rain
Wind us your winds—of course we'll complain.
But leave us alive with reason to sing
When you are done chastening, chastening.

—John Barr

HURRICANE, ANTIGUA, WEST INDIES

Wildfire

It's the earth I'm after,
the pungent taste of soil
sifted over time,
seasoned with moss and dried leaves,
perfectly stirred by
the undulation of worm.
I am grateful for the lightning
that struck the first tree
like a match.
I grew giddy,
my blue tongue licking
grass, timber, those strange boxes
men live in.
I rushed red, greedily devouring
all that stood between me
and the sweet delicacy of Earth.
And when only we two remained,
I licked her warm skin,
finally content to simmer,
to lie low, to die.

—Nikki Grimes

FOREST FIRE, CUSTER STATE PARK, SOUTH DAKOTA, U.S.A.

 *in distress*

Flood

Your levees break
   And overflow
Like promises
   Made long ago.

The city stop
   Signs disappear,
Black water crests
   At level: **FEAR.**

Old family photos
   Float away
With furniture
   And yesterday.

Then come the tears
   Like rivulets:
A Mississippi
   Of regrets.

     —Peter Kostin

IN SEA

SON

When It Is
Snowing

When it is snowing
the blue jay
is the only piece of
sky
in my
backyard.

—Siv Cedering

BLUE JAY

Storm Ending

Thunder blossoms gorgeously above our heads,
Great, hollow, bell-like flowers,
Rumbling in the wind,
Stretching clappers to strike our ears . . .
Full-lipped flowers
Bitten by the sun
Bleeding rain
Dripping rain like golden honey—
And the sweet earth flying from the thunder.

—Jean Toomer

You Never Hear the Garden Grow

Row on row,
you never hear the garden
grow.

Seeds split.
Roots shove and reach.
Earth heaves.

Leaves unfurl.
Stems pierce the
ground.

Peapods fatten.
Vines
stretch and curl.

Such growing
going on
without a sound!

—*Lilian Moore*

PEA PODS

135

here is a poem
of love and hope:

from a cold
de cem ber
a f t e r n o o n
out here in the flatland of e a s t ohio
and i am o u t in this considerable yard
u n d e r this h e a v y grey sky
pre s s ing on to my s h o u l d e r s
and s w e e t w o m a n
my head is bending l o w as the song goes
and my eyes are fixed on frozen patches of past
and future loves and deaths and dis re gards
and i am l i v i n g into my eight i eth y e a r
and i still address these poems to you to y o u r
eyes to that always welcoming smile to those
w e l c o m i n g a r m s

i am stripping away all that is not necessary
and this has been my p l a n m y pro cess
for m o s t of my conscious l i f e out here
discerning what is alive and what is almost
worth the mouth to mouth of the h e a r t
and i still believe in the power and force of love
as i can almost feel the land s h a k i n g with
the power and force of mindful des truc t i o n
and i shake under the daily drumbeat of death

please r e a d this poem with your o w n power and l o v e
and smile and r e r e a d and nod and be angry with resolve
these s t r u g g l e s must continue through h a r d w i n t e r
as we prepare for the new and g r e e n i n g spring

—a r n o l d a d o f f

frost

How does
The plain
Transparency
Of water

Sprout these
Lacy fronds
And plumes
And tendrils?

And where,
Before window-
Panes, did
They root

Their lush
Crystal forests,
Their cold
Silver jungles?

—*Valerie Worth*

April Rain Song

Let the rain kiss you.
Let the rain beat upon your head with silver liquid drops.
Let the rain sing you a lullaby.

The rain makes still pools on the sidewalk.
The rain makes running pools in the gutter.
The rain plays a little sleep-song on our roof at night—

And I love the rain.

—Langston Hughes

JAPANESE TREE FROG

Metamorphosis

Dandelion!
Lowly, brilliant, friend of mine.
You bloom in grass,
through gravel, cracks,
stand alone or bunch in packs.
Stubborn, spindly, tell me why
you stretch your yellow toward the sky,
until you, furry, turn to seed,
come undone, let loose, and fly.

—Sara Holbrook

I So Liked Spring

I so liked Spring last year
    Because you were here;—
        The thrushes too—
Because it was these you so liked to hear—
    I so liked you.

This year's a different thing,—
    I'll not think of you.
But I'll like Spring because it is simply Spring
    As the thrushes do.

—Charlotte Mew

Why Leaves
Change Color in the Fall

I was just about
to explain to the class that leaves
are nature's food factories taking water from the
ground and carbon dioxide from the air and using
sunlight to turn water and carbon dioxide into glucose
a kind of sugar that gives a tree its high energy through a
process called photosynthesis which is helped along by
a chemical known as chlorophyll that makes trees and plants
green though during autumn photosynthesis does not work
as efficiently due to less water and shorter hours of daylight so
trees begin to shut down their manufacturing and green
chlorophyll-filled leaves take a holiday by turning
themselves yellow and orange or like that sugar maple
for instance where the glucose trapped in the leaves
now that photosynthesis has stopped begins to turn
into an eye-delightful scarlet . . . but then I
thought why take the time to explain it
when they could all just sit here
with me to watch
that old tree
H o u d i n i
pull another
color   trick
and send the
leaves   like
feathers of a
dove falling softly
t o   t h e   g r o u n d

—J. Patrick Lewis

CANADIAN GEESE

Something Told the Wild Geese

Something told the wild geese
   It was time to go.
Though the fields lay golden
   Something whispered,—"Snow."

Leaves were green and stirring,
   Berries, luster-glossed,
But beneath warm feathers
   Something cautioned,—"Frost."

All the sagging orchards
   Steamed with amber spice,
But each wild breast stiffened
   At remembered ice.

Something told the wild geese
   It was time to fly,—
Summer sun was on their wings,
   Winter in their cry.

—Rachel Field

February Tale

Above the earth
it's mitten-cold,
and children scurry,
rubber-soled.
Their icy breath
curls in the air
and every tree
is twig-thin bare . . .

Oh, February.

Yet far beneath
the frozen crust,
an eager bud
begins to thrust.
Another season's
written there;
another story,
winter's heir . . .

Ah, February!

—*Renée M. LaTulippe*

Sounds of Winter

The Old October Ogres come
without a fee-fi-fo or fum:
They lumber in *tum-tum-ti-tum.*

Nesting in trees forty feet tall,
they shake the leaves that fall in fall—
you hardly notice them at all.

But soon you hear the muffled snores
of Dark December Dinosaurs,
who wake to make the wind that roars,

The frost that bites, the ice that numbs,
the fee-fi-foes and dreadful fums . . .
when Ogres go and winter comes.

—*Anonymous*

SIBILLINI NATIONAL PARK, UMBRIA, ITALY

November

The bottoms of autumn
wear diamonds of frost;
the tops of the trees rue
the sweaters they've lost.

Red squirrels, busy packing
oak cupboards for weeks,
still rattle their branches
with seeds in their cheeks.

Gray clouds go on promising
winter's first storm
while we stay inside by
the fire to keep warm.

Home biscuits are baking,
the gravy is stirred,
two pumpkin pies cool
by the thank-you bird.

—*Mariel Bede*

EURASIAN RED SQUIRREL

Autumn

A touch of cold in the Autumn night—
I walked abroad,
And saw the ruddy moon lean over a hedge
Like a red-faced farmer.
I did not stop to speak, but nodded,
And round about were the wistful stars
With white faces like town children.

—*T. E. Hulme*

FULL MOON

November Night

Listen . . .
With faint dry sound,
Like steps of passing ghosts,
The leaves, frost-crisp'd, break from the trees
And fall.

—*Adelaide Crapsey*

FROSTED MAPLE LEAVES

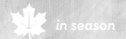

A Crack
in the Clouds

How could
one slight
slit,
just a tiny bit
of a crack
in the cover
of clouds,
permit
such a pouring of sun
that engulfs
E V E R Y O N E ?

—*Constance Levy*

SMERILLO, ITALY

In Just

in Just-
spring   when the world is mud-
luscious the little
lame balloonman

whistles   far   and wee

and eddieandbill come
running from marbles and
piracies and it's
spring

when the world is puddle-wonderful

the queer
old balloonman whistles
far   and   wee
and bettyandisbel come dancing

from hop-scotch and jump-rope and

it's
spring
and
        the

                goat-footed

balloonMan   whistles
far
and
wee

                —*e. e. cummings*

The Pasture

I'm going out to clean the pasture spring;
I'll only stop to rake the leaves away
(And wait to watch the water clear, I may):
I sha'n't be gone long.—You come too.

I'm going out to fetch the little calf
That's standing by the mother. It's so young,
It totters when she licks it with her tongue.
I sha'n't be gone long.—You come too.

—Robert Frost

My Heart Leaps Up

My heart leaps up when I behold
   A rainbow in the sky:
So was it when my life began;
So is it now I am a man;
So be it when I shall grow old,
   Or let me die!
The Child is father of the Man;
And I could wish my days to be
Bound each to each by natural piety.

—William Wordsworth

For All

Ah to be alive
on a mid-September morn
fording a stream
barefoot, pants rolled up,
holding boots, pack on,
sunshine, ice in the shallows,
northern rockies.

Rustle and shimmer of icy creek waters
stones turn underfoot, small and hard as toes
cold nose dripping
singing inside
creek music, heart music,
smell of sun on gravel.

I pledge allegiance

I pledge allegiance to the soil
of Turtle Island,
and to the beings who thereon dwell

one ecosystem
in diversity
under the sun
with joyful interpenetration for all.

—*Gary Snyder*

The *LONG* Summer

Then summer sat and smiled
As though to stay all year,
But then I was a child.

Now, given to good cheer
And glad to be beguiled,
I stay a child all year.

—*James Hayford*

IN SPLE

GRAND PRISMATIC POOL, WYOMING, U.S.A.

NDOR

GREAT BARRIER REEF MARINE PARK, QUEENSLAND, AUSTRALIA

The Great Barrier Reef

In the Coral Sea, off the coast of Queensland, Australia

It's sixteen hundred miles long
along the Queensland coast,
the barrier reef whose name is "Great,"
and that's no idle boast.

It's sixteen hundred miles long
and every inch alive.
Perhaps you'd like to have a look?
You do not need to dive

or even get your swimsuit wet
to see this awesome place;
the reef's so huge it's visible
by astronauts in space.

To think, you can be orbiting
the earth while looking at
a teeming turtle, dolphin, whale
and porpoise habitat.

Your eyes will tell the story
and you will not doubt its moral:
There's hardly anything on earth
more beautiful than coral.

—Robert Schechter

Mammatus Clouds

Thunder coming with its usual heavy hammer
   and the sky strange, bubbled
   with clouds, the air humming
   and warning us away.
Tornado coming today with its terrible trouble
   and the sky pouched,
   pockets of ice and water waiting
   for their own best moment to burst.
Hard weather coming, for the worst reasons:
   warm air, cool air, thermal instability,
   wind shear, sublimation—
   we cotton to the calmest explanations.
Something coming. Could be okay, could be misery—
   who knows which or why?
   Look at that sky, filled with question marks,
   every mark cloud a mystery.

—Julie Larios

MAMMATUS CLOUDS, OKLAHOMA, U.S.A.

Moonbow at Cumberland Falls

In southeastern Kentucky, U.S.A.

Moonbow, moonbow made of mist and moonglow where the river flows over the falls
Full moon's moonshow how colors inside light glow where Cumberland cascades into falls
Red, orange, yellow, green waver on mist's silver screen where land level drops and river falls
Blue indigoes to violet where rivermist and moonbeam net Mystery among us yet:
Moonbow at Cumberland Falls

—George Ella Lyon

Solar **Eclipse**

And owlets know it's nearing.
And hounds pretend it's night.
And Sun comes crowned in her corona.
    Stare—
    She'll steal
    Your sight.

And moonflowers yawn their petals.
And morning glories bind.
And earthworms glimmer in the gardens.
    Beware—
    She'll glare
    You blind.

        —Steven Withrow

SOLAR ECLIPSE

Fish Rain

Animal rain is an extremely rare
meteorological phenomenon.
Once in a weird while, it rains animals.
Not cats and dogs, but toads and frogs, always
the same species, and always the same size.
The most rained animals are tiny fish.
What makes live fish fall out of thunderclouds
many miles away from the nearest lake?
Are they whooshed up by fierce tornadic winds?

It has rained fish in Australia, India,
Louisiana, and Saskatchewan.
And in Yoro, a town in Honduras,
fish rain falls one or two times every year.
They celebrate it with a festival
thanking the fish rain for feeding the poor.
You'll probably never walk in a fish rain.
But, just in case, remember if you do,
to carry your umbrella upside down!

        —Marilyn Nelson

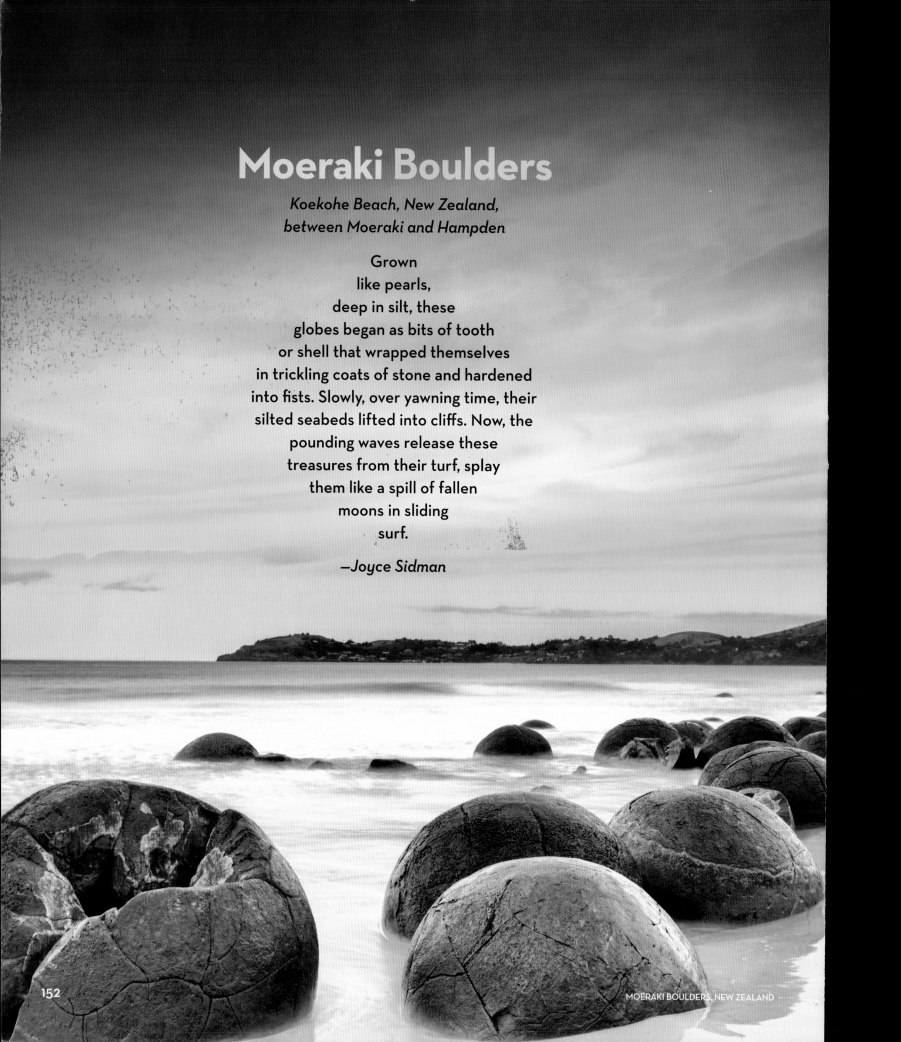

Moeraki Boulders

Koekohe Beach, New Zealand,
between Moeraki and Hampden

Grown
like pearls,
deep in silt, these
globes began as bits of tooth
or shell that wrapped themselves
in trickling coats of stone and hardened
into fists. Slowly, over yawning time, their
silted seabeds lifted into cliffs. Now, the
pounding waves release these
treasures from their turf, splay
them like a spill of fallen
moons in sliding
surf.

—Joyce Sidman

MOERAKI BOULDERS, NEW ZEALAND

BADLANDS NATIONAL MONUMENT, SOUTH DAKOTA, U.S.A.

Fossil Beds at the Badlands

Badlands National Park, South Dakota, U.S.A.

Pass the RUSH-NO-MORE CAMPGROUND,
take a few turns, absorb the jagged shapes.
Saber-toothed cats sleeping,
wild horse dreams pressed into rock.
No quiet bigger than theirs.
Step gently, touch nothing,
does anyone remember?
Once they roamed the land of shining grasses,
owning sky. Tonight there's a bighorn sheep,
his back to the sunset, prairie dogs huddling
underground. How does so much disappear?

This kingdom holds lost hopes.
They are orange now. Some look like
fingers pointing to the sky.
Drop your own pain, no one will know.
Navigate soft sediment, whispering *Rhino.*
Everyone's emptiness made elegant,
even the bison and black-footed ferret,
even the woman, even the man.

—*Naomi Shihab Nye*

153

INGLEBOROUGH MOUNTAIN, UK

SUN HALO

154

Glacial Erratic

Big Rock, 15,000 tons, Alberta,
Canada, and elsewhere

An open field surrounds a boulder so big, no

Giant could carry or move it. Who could have
Lifted it? Who set it down? Old people say it has
Always been here. Older than memory—
Could that be true? How did it get here, and why
Is it different from all other rocks for miles around?
Every mystery seeks its answer. See how this one,
Receding, drops a poem onto the field of this page.

—Helen Frost

Sun Dogs

The sun made a special appearance
on his balcony, above the crowd,
surrounded by a halo
of diamond dust and clouds.

On either side of him there stood
two sun dogs, north and south,
keeping almost silent guard,
growls slipping from their mouths.

When the sun excused his audience
and disappeared in the dark,

he dismissed the sun dogs,
one and two, to guard the city parks.

—Janet S. Wong

Catatumbo LIGHTNING

*Observed only over the mouth of the
Catatumbo River where it empties into
Lake Maracaibo, Venezuela*

It is impossible to describe,
impossible to believe even as you see it—
the entire night sky awash in crackling light,

arc upon arc, cloud to cloud, sky to earth,
each bolt a jolt of energy enough
to power a small village

like the one on stilts in the marshes
of Lake Maracaibo, where topography
and the gods conspire to produce

near-nightly light shows—half mad science,
half Mother Nature—enough
to stop anyone in their tracks,

including Sir Francis Drake, retreating
all those years ago, his invasion revealed
by a Catatumbo lightning cannonade.

Did Drake gaze skyward, slack-jawed
as he sailed? Was he dumbstruck?
Was he weak-kneed with wonder?

Or did he curse his fate,
rent by lightning and thunder?

—Kelly Ramsdell Fineman

The **Mariana Trench**

*Western Pacific Ocean,
east of the Mariana Islands*

In all the oceans, nowhere else so deep,
So dark with secrets men won't let it keep:
It yields to human eyes in submarines
And then, full of itself, goes back to sleep.

You wouldn't dream that hidden at its core
Life would go on as it has done for more
Than most of time, though seven heavy miles
Of water press down upon its floor.

To fathom it at last, to put on show
All that it holds, laid out in a neat row,
May happen sooner than to do that to
The mind of someone whom you think you know.

—*X. J. Kennedy*

The Grand Canyon

Carved out by the Colorado River,
Arizona, U.S.A.

Arriving, I felt I'd come to a place of power:
a holy place—
just as Pueblo people must have felt
so many years ago
drawn to that massive burnt sienna otherness:
that unimaginable hugeness
where layer after layer of stone
authored a geologic history book
going back, back in time
millions of years—
plunging down, down below the plateau
down below sea level.
In spite of knowing the canyon
was the work of the Colorado River,
I could imagine some Gulliver, some Colossus,
hands hennaed, the color of clay,
resting on the canyon's distant rim,
resting after creating his masterpiece.

—*Bobbi Katz*

MOUNT EVEREST, CHINA-NEPAL

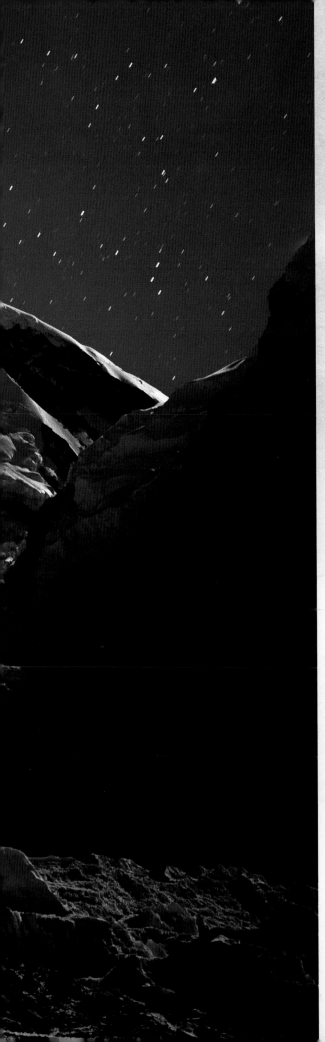

Mount Everest

Earth's tallest mountain, located on the border of Nepal
and China in southern Asia, adds to its height each year.

Mount Everest calls out to the quiet stars,

"I am stronger than the wind,
I am immense,
noble,
King of the World!

As I lift my huge weight high, high above,
I see how tiny earth is.

Deeper and deeper into enormous spaces
I will climb and lay my shadow on all of it, everything.

Men call me 'Holy'
for I sail the skies,
and have now reached the crossing point
of heaven and earth . . .
                              I am coming!"

The Universe arches over,
and the stars, bending low,
whisper,
"We are waiting."

                              —Deborah Chandra

LAKE HILLIER, AUSTRALIA

Pink Lake

Middle Island,
Recherche Archipelago,
Western Australia

No natural site is sillier
than rosy-hued Lake Hillier.
You wouldn't be the first to think,
"This can't be real. That lake is pink!"
You'd not be first to ask, "How come
Lake Hillier looks like bubble gum?"
Ten times the salt found in the sea,
its waters are a mystery.

The tint may owe its genesis
to algae photosynthesis
which turns pink to attract sunlight.

But just in case that isn't right—
perhaps pink microbes halophilic,
who find salt water most idyllic,
have gathered in a massive group,
creating cotton candy soup.

Either one would cause the lake
to look like a strawberry shake.
You might be disappointed, though;
to find out we don't really know.
Salty Lake Hillier: Pink sensation.
Australian Barbie's dream vacation.
A pigment of imagination.

—*Allan Wolf*

160

Brinicle

Arctic Ocean,
dark, vast
water cave guarded by an
arc of sea ice above

Ceiling recedes,
feeds salt to the deep
Super-saltwater ribbon flows,
grows, and sinks

Stalactite
with a frigid core
wears a crystal
cloak of ice

Brinicle gushes,
rushing down to the
seafloor,
an icy finger of death

      —Laura Purdie Salas

BRINICLES, ROSS SEA, ANTARCTICA

Antelope Canyon

On Navajo land, Page, Arizona, U.S.A.

For millions of years, water sculpted this sandstone,
　　winding and swirling around rocks, waterfalls
buffed sharp corners into curves,
　　careened around boulders,
crashing in flash floods, torrents gushing,
　　polishing as they roiled and plunged, their force scraping
　　　smooth canyons and round gold openings,
　　　　sunlight descending in beams,
　　columns rising, clouds bursting,
dark crevices echoing water's roar,
　　for millions of years,

dry seasons, streambeds silent
　　　　snowflakes falling into the spirals,
　　and then the slow melting,
pronghorn antelope licking spring stars at sunset.

—Pat Mora

Rainforest

The forest drips and glows with green.
The tree-frog croaks his far-off song.
His voice is stillness, moss and rain
drunk from the forest ages long.

We cannot understand that call
unless we move into his dream,
where all is one and one is all
and frog and python are the same.

We with our quick dividing eyes
measure, distinguish and are gone.
The forest burns, the tree-frog dies,
yet one is all and all are one.

—Judith Wright

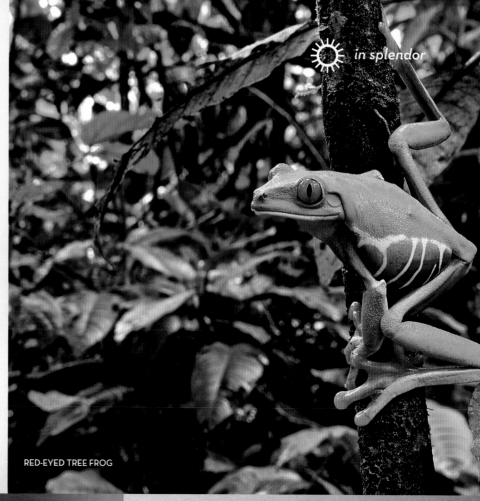

in splendor

RED-EYED TREE FROG

Niagara Falls

Between the province of Ontario, Canada, and the state of New York, U.S.A.

What a stage! What a play!
Thunder at its birth.
The longest running show around:
the greatest hit on earth.

USA and Canada
co-host this smashing show.
Don't miss the mist that nature kissed,
where double rainbows grow.

—Avis Harley

Yellowstone

Northwest Wyoming, U.S.A.

Forget all your troubles.
Forget all your cares.
And go to the park
With bisons and bears.
Moose go grazing.
Gray wolves stalk.
Great elk climb,
And pronghorn walk.
Rivers flow
And geysers spout.
Fir trees rise,
And lilies sprout.
Brown trout swim
And falcons fly.
All beneath a
Big Blue Sky.

—Douglas Florian

BISON, YELLOWSTONE NATIONAL PARK, WYOMING, U.S.A.

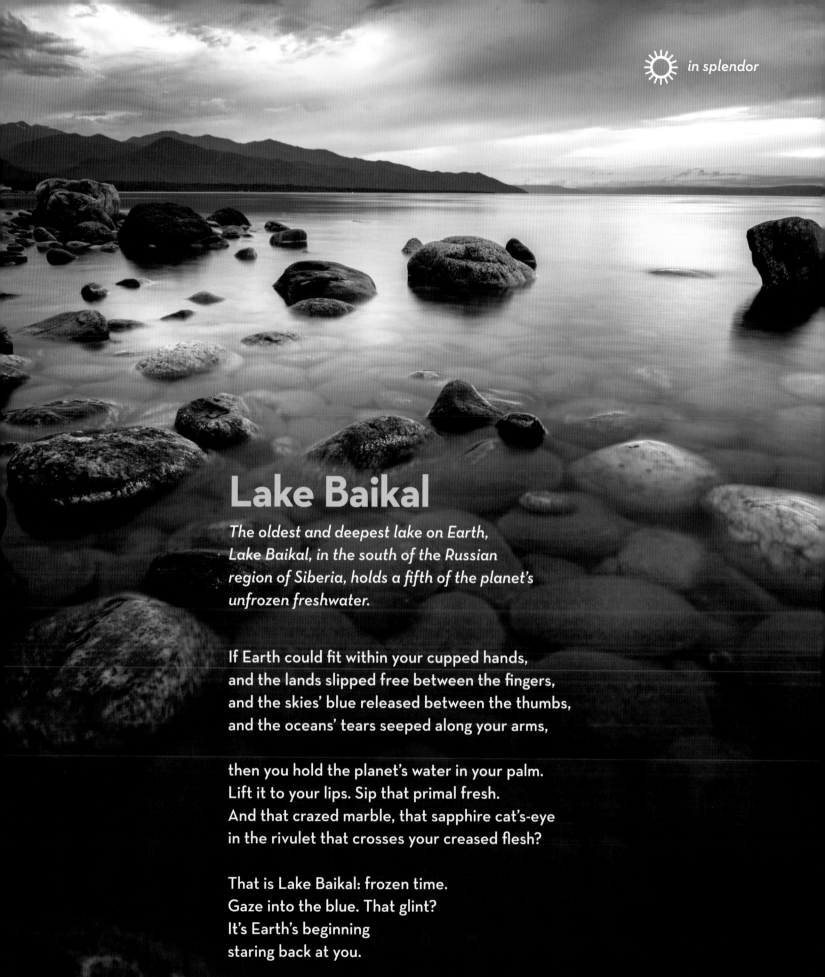

Lake Baikal

The oldest and deepest lake on Earth,
Lake Baikal, in the south of the Russian
region of Siberia, holds a fifth of the planet's
unfrozen freshwater.

If Earth could fit within your cupped hands,
and the lands slipped free between the fingers,
and the skies' blue released between the thumbs,
and the oceans' tears seeped along your arms,

then you hold the planet's water in your palm.
Lift it to your lips. Sip that primal fresh.
And that crazed marble, that sapphire cat's-eye
in the rivulet that crosses your creased flesh?

That is Lake Baikal: frozen time.
Gaze into the blue. That glint?
It's Earth's beginning
staring back at you.

—Michael J. Rosen

LAKE BAIKAL, RUSSIA

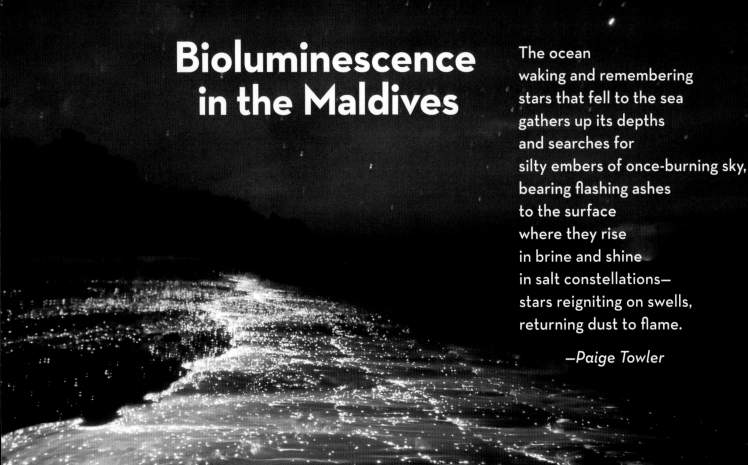

Bioluminescence in the Maldives

The ocean
waking and remembering
stars that fell to the sea
gathers up its depths
and searches for
silty embers of once-burning sky,
bearing flashing ashes
to the surface
where they rise
in brine and shine
in salt constellations—
stars reigniting on swells,
returning dust to flame.

—Paige Towler

BIOLUMINESCENT PLANKTON, MALDIVES

Pororoca
Tidal Bore

*Araguari Pororoca,
Amapá state, Brazil*

The Pororoca Tidal Bore
is the ocean at war with the river,
waves twice as tall as tanks
rolling, rumbling, roaring up the Amazon
delivering blast after blast after blast—

It lasts only days each year.
Ordinary people scurry away in fear
while surfers crazed as soldiers
surface from nowhere, eager
to navigate the battlefield of debris.

Trees: torpedoes. Rocks: grenades.
They choke on mud but they don't care.
When the *lunático* power of the pororoca
dissolves into nothing, these surfer-soldiers
will stuff their packs and head back home.

—Janet S. Wong

Wonder Down Under

Uluru (Ayers Rock), Australia

I'm known around the rockin' world by many,
enchanted by my ruddy, wrinkled dome.
But neighbors of my ilk? I don't have any.
The harsh and empty outback is my home.
My power is mysterious and mythic.
My people, the Anangu, understand
that I am more than simply monolithic—
I am a huge Australian rock star in the sand.

And though I love your awe and admiration,
applaud me from a distance, if you will.
I'm big enough for long-range observation,
and I can guarantee you'll get a thrill.
In photos or in person you will gawk,

even if you're not a fan of rock.

—*Ted Scheu*

ULURU (AYERS ROCK), ULURU-KATA TJUTA NATIONAL PARK, AUSTRALIA

Red Tide

What if a tiny shred of alga,
a prosaic, single-celled seaweed,

which no one hears, no one sees,
a nothing caught in the Red Tide of life,

what if instead of wallowing in waves like a gutless jellyfish,
this helpless kelp gets a grand idea of its own,

if this lone wolf, this powerless thing,
bands together with other plankton in protest?

What if by day
the waters bleed,

and under the moon suddenly seen,
each alga burns blue-green,

now the machine of Algae United
waving its bioluminescent flag.

                    —April Halprin Wayland

TORREY PINES STATE BEACH, CALIFORNIA, U.S.A.

in splendor

Petrified Forest

*Navajo and Apache Counties,
northeastern Arizona, U.S.A.*

This is a place
where trees were buried.
This is a place
where water crept in.
This is a place
where minerals stayed—
where a stone tree looks
like a wood tree's twin.

Now the wood is gone
but the bark remains.
Rings of quartz spin
round and round.
These rainbow logs
that once were trees
tell ancient tales
without a sound.

—*Amy Ludwig VanDerwater*

PETRIFIED WOOD

169

Aurora Borealis

Over the shores of Labrador
a certain rippling purple curtain
scatters light throughout the night.
(Wait—the color's now a duller
hue of violet-turning-blue!)
This arctic veil, a breaching whale
could peer behind, and still be blind
as anyone. The northern sun
has bent to drape her gauzy cape
across the skies, and left my eyes
to stare and stare at the glittering air.

—Steven Withrow

 *in splendor*

Northern Lights

As self-absorbed and callow as a teen,
He never gave a thought to purple, blue,
Pink, red—or any color in between.

Amusements would appear but they were few
Till August heaved an easel in the sky
And *color*, modulating into *hue*,

Flew summer's spectral spectacle on high.

—*J. Patrick Lewis*

AURORA BOREALIS

171

Nothing Gold Can Stay

Nature's first green is gold,
Her hardest hue to hold.
Her early leaf's a flower;
But only so an hour.
Then leaf subsides to leaf.
So Eden sank to grief,
So dawn goes down to day.
Nothing gold can stay.

—*Robert Frost*

LAST

Nature

O Nature! I do not aspire
To be the highest in thy choir, —
To be a meteor in thy sky,
Or comet that may range on high;
Only a zephyr that may blow
Among the reeds by the river low;
Give me thy most privy place
Where to run my airy race.

In some withdrawn, unpublic mead
Let me sigh upon a reed,
Or in the woods, with leafy din,
Whisper the still evening in:
Some still work give me to do, —
Only—be it near to you!

For I'd rather be thy child
And pupil, in the forest wild,

Than be the king of men elsewhere,
And most sovereign slave of care;
To have one moment of thy dawn,
Than share the city's year forlorn.

—Henry David Thoreau

THOUGHTS

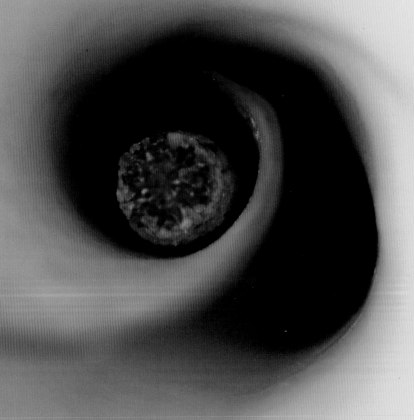

Swift Things Are Beautiful

Swift things are beautiful:
Swallows and deer,
And lightning that falls
Bright veined and clear,
Rivers and meteors,
Wind in the wheat,
The strong-withered horse,
The runner's sure feet.

And slow things are beautiful:
The closing of day,
The pause of the wave
That curves downward to spray,
The ember that crumbles,
The opening flower,
And the ox that moves on
In the quiet of power.

—*Elizabeth Coatsworth*

Lessons of
Nature

After Samuel Hazo

The darker the night, the wiser the owl.
The faster the hare, the smarter the fox.
The plumper the bird, the quicker the snake.
The hotter the day, the louder the bee.

The brighter the sun, the gladder the rose.
The stiffer the wind, the stiller the hawk.
The finer the flake, the lighter the snow.
The denser the fog, the thinner the tree.

The wetter the rain, the greener the frog.
The drier the field, the sadder the corn.
The higher the peak, the colder the air.
The deeper the gorge, the older the land.

The blacker the cloud, the whiter the wave.
The madder the sky, the fiercer the storm.
The flatter the sea, the sweeter the beach.
The farther the tide, the harder the sand.

—*J. Patrick Lewis*

the earth
is a living thing

is a black shambling bear
ruffling its wild back and tossing
mountains into the sea

is a black hawk circling
the burying ground circling the bones
picked clean and discarded

is a fish black blind in the belly of water
is a diamond blind in the black belly of coal

is a black and living thing
is a favorite child
of the universe
feel her rolling her hand
in its kinky hair
feel her brushing it clean

—*Lucille Clifton*

In Beauty May I Walk

In beauty may I walk
All day long may I walk
Through the returning seasons may I walk
Beautifully will I possess again
Beautifully birds
Beautifully joyful birds
On the trail marked with pollen may I walk
With grasshoppers about my feet may I walk
With dew about my feet may I walk
With beauty may I walk
With beauty before me may I walk
With beauty behind me may I walk
With beauty above me may I walk
With beauty all around me may I walk
In old age, wandering on a trail of beauty, lively, may I walk
In old age, wandering on a trail of beauty, living again, may I walk
It is finished in beauty
It is finished in beauty

—Anonymous (Navajo Indian)

Post-it Notes
From the World

Is sadness the reason
for rainbows?

Are gardens why people
have knees?

Are bluebirds why houses
have windows?

Are geese the inventors
of V's?

A drought is the rain's inspiration;
a flood is a river's despair.

The sun is a storm on vacation.

A rose is a gift to the air.

The sky's a high-fashion designer.

The ocean's a bowl of fish soup.

Blue whale was the first ocean liner.

And seagulls made up the
word *swoop*.

Snowflakes are the
world's art collection.

Full moon's a firefly to the stars.

A canyon's a flatland's correction.

The wind's just a gust of guitars.

An orchard's the reason for ladders.

The tallest trees laugh at a stair.

A weed is indeed a
misunderstood seed.

But a rose, oh a rose
always wins
by a nose,
a rose is a gift to the air.

Would tides
like to skip daily practice
at filling the shore's hourglass?

Are porcupines cousins to cactus?

Are jellyfish breakable glass?

—*J. Patrick Lewis*

who is mother nature?

When Mother Nature's near—in waterfalls, rivers, rainbows, meadows, or oceans—her admirers react with love, awe, curiosity, even fear, if she decides to reveal her grumpier side. The lady can be seen through telescopes or microscopes, from mountaintops or ravines, with the wind in our hair, soil in our hands, or sand in our toes. For those who aren't hopelessly city-bound, looking out a window will do.

Driven to explore the *science* behind the wonder of it all, Charles Darwin filled scores of notebooks about what was then the unexplored wildlife of the Galápagos Islands. Countless nature writers have followed his courageous example. Others have put themselves in nature, like naturalist John Muir, who once rode out a northern American windstorm by cocooning himself in the branches of a sky-high Douglas spruce. (Muir is famous—or should be—for saying, "The clearest way into the Universe is through a forest wilderness.")

Some humans, however, have no use for wild places, a view once expressed by Woody Allen with his typical wit: "I love nature. I just don't want to get any of it on me." For some, their love for animals extends only as far as Fido or Sweet Pea. That we share the Earth equally with other creatures is a notion as foreign and irrelevant to them as the disappearance of the rain forests or the melting of the ice caps.

But Mother Nature doesn't care who likes her. Nor is she bothered about being ignored. A midwife at the birth of creatures large and small, she will go on making waves by making waves, assembling forests, flowering deserts, and beautifying gardens. We can embrace her or resist her charms; it is of no concern to her.

Who is the mysterious lady known as Mother Nature? She is the material world, the environment of trees, plants, animals, everything under and over the sun. In short, she equals the world around us and includes whatever is not built by human hands.

Mother Nature is where we live. In other words, she is
a refuge to the lost,
a magnet to the curious,
a dare to the daring,
the cradle of rapture,
the university of the universe,
the glory of a morning and of a morning-glory,
not a whale but the idea of a whale,
a sign rewriter: I Welcome All No Trespassing,
the best cure for couch disease,
an opera performed by birds, bullfrogs on drums,
the sound of silence . . . amplified
to the symphony of the spheres, and _____
_____ .

Can you add another short description of Mother Nature to this poem?

The poets and photographers who have come together to produce National Geographic's *Book of Nature Poetry* would agree with John Keats, who defined their abiding faith: "The poetry of earth is never dead."

resources

Here is a selected bibliography of children's books on wordplay in poetry that you might find especially useful as you explore your own paths to poetry.

ACROSTICS

Harley, Avis. *African Acrostics: A Word in Edgeways.* Candlewick, 2009.

Schnur, Steven. *Autumn: An Alphabet Acrostic.* Clarion, 1997. (See also his Winter, Spring, and Summer acrostic books in this series.)

ANAGRAMS

Lederer, Richard. *The Circus of Words.* Chicago Review Press, 2001.

Raczka, Bob. *Lemonade: and Other Poems Squeezed From a Single Word.* Roaring Brook, 2011.

DOUBLE DACTYLS, OR IF YOU PREFER, HIGGLEDY-PIGGLEDYS

Hecht, Anthony, and John Hollander, eds. *Jiggery Pokery: A Compendium of Double Dactyls.* Atheneum, 1967.

EPITAPHS

Lewis, J. Patrick. *Once Upon a Tomb: Gravely Humorous Verses.* Candlewick, 2006.

Lewis, J. Patrick, and Jane Yolen. *Last Laughs: Animal Epitaphs.* Charlesbridge, 2012.

Yolen, Jane, and J. Patrick Lewis. *Last Laughs: Prehistoric Epitaphs.* Charlesbridge, 2015.

HAIKU

Farrar, Sid. *The Year Comes Round: Haiku Through the Seasons.* Albert Whitman, 2012.

George, Kristine O'Connell. *Fold Me a Poem.* Harcourt, 2005.

Issa, Kobayashi. *Today and Today.* Scholastic, 2007.

Mora, Pat. *Yum! Mmm! Qué Rico! Americas' Sproutings.* Lee & Low, 2007.

Prelutsky, Jack. *If Not for the Cat: Haiku.* Greenwillow, 2004.

Raczka, Bob. *Guyku: A Year of Haiku for Boys.* Houghton Mifflin Harcourt, 2010.

Rosen, Michael J. *The Cuckoo's Haiku and Other Birding Poems.* Candlewick, 2009.

_____ . *The Hound Dog's Haiku and Other Poems for Dog Lovers.* Candlewick, 2011.

Snyder, Betsy. *I Haiku You.* Random House, 2012.

Wardlaw, Lee. *Won Ton: A Cat Tale Told in Haiku.* Henry Holt, 2011.

Yolen, Jane. *Least Things: Poems About Small Natures.* Wordsong/Boyds Mills, 2003.

Ziefert, Harriet. *Hanukkah Haiku.* Blue Apple Books, 2008.

LIPOGRAMS

Lawson, JonArno. *A Voweller's Bestiary.* Porcupine's Quill, 2008.

LITTLE WILLIES

Invented by Harry Graham, showcased by X. J. Kennedy in his *Brats* books.

PALINDROMES

Agee, Jon. *Go, Hang a Salami! I'm a Lasagna Hog! And Other Palindromes.* Farrar, Straus, Giroux, 1994. (See also the other books in this series.)

PARODIES

Levine, Gail Carson. *Forgive Me, I Meant to Do It: False Apology Poems.* HarperCollins, 2012.

Shapiro, Karen Jo. *I Must Go Down to the Beach Again.* Charlesbridge, 2007.

Sidman, Joyce. *This Is Just to Say: Poems of Apology and Forgiveness.* Houghton Mifflin, 2007.

PORTMANTEAUS

Prelutsky, Jack. *Scranimals.* HarperCollins, 2002.

_____ . *Behold the Bold Umbrellaphant.* Greenwillow, 2006.

_____ . *Stardines Swim High Across the Sky.* Greenwillow, 2013.

resources

CONTINUED

REBUSES

Calmenson, Stephanie. *Kindergarten Kids: Riddles, Rebuses, Wiggles, Giggles, and More!* HarperCollins, 2005.

Lewis, J. Patrick. *The Fantastitc 5&10 Cent Store.* Schwartz & Wade/Random House, 2010.

REVERSOS

Singer, Marilyn. *Mirror, Mirror.* Dutton, 2010.

_____ . *Follow, Follow.* Dutton, 2013.

SHAPED POEMS

Franco, Betsy. *A Curious Collection of Cats.* Tricycle Press, 2009.

_____ . *A Dazzling Display of Dogs.* Tricycle Press, 2011.

Graham, Joan Bransfield. Splish Splash. Houghton Mifflin, 2001.

_____ . *Flicker Flash.* Houghton Mifflin, 2003.

Grandits, John. Technically, It's Not My Fault. Sandpiper, 2004.

_____ . *Blue Lipstick: Concrete Poems.* Clarion, 2007.

Janeczko, Paul B., ed. *A Poke in the I.* Candlewick, 2001.

Lewis, J. Patrick. *Doodle Dandies.* Atheneum, 1998.

Magee, Wes, ed. *Madtail, Miniwhale and Other Shape Poems.* Puffin, 1989.

Roemer, Heidi. *Come to My Party and Other Shape Poems.* Henry Holt, 2004.

Sidman, Joyce. *Meow Ruff: A Story in Concrete Poetry.* Houghton Mifflin, 2007.

SPOONERISMS

Silverstein, Shel. *Runny Babbitt: A Billy Sook.* HarperCollins, 2005.

TONGUE TWISTERS

Agee, Jon. *Orangutan Tongs.* Hyperion, 2009.

ALL FORMS

Espy, Willard R. *A Children's Almanac of Words at Play.* Clarkson N. Potter, 1982.

Franco, Betsy. *Conversations With a Poet: Inviting Poetry Into K–12 Classrooms.* Richard C. Owen, 2005.

Graham, Joan Bransfield. *The Poem That Will Not End.* Two Lions, 2014.

Harley, Avis. *Fly With Poetry: An ABC of Poetry.* Wordsong, 2000.

_____ . *Leap Into Poetry: More ABC's of Poetry.* Wordsong, 2001.

Janeczko, Paul B. *Poetry From A to Z: A Guide for Young Writers.* Bradbury, 1994.

_____ . *A Kick in the Head.* Candlewick, 2005.

Kennedy, X. J., and Dorothy Kennedy. *Knock at a Star: A Child's Introduction to Poetry.* Revised ed. Little, Brown, 1999.

Livingston, Myra Cohn. *Poem-Making: Ways to Begin Writing Poetry.* HarperCollins, 1991.

CHRISTMAS ISLAND RED CRAB

index

TITLE INDEX

POET INDEX

index

FIRST LINE INDEX

SUBJECT INDEX
Boldface indicates illustrations.

text credits

6. **The Thing Is the Thing Is Green,** Peggy Gifford. From *The Great Big Green* by Peggy Gifford. Copyright © by Peggy Gifford. Published by Boyds Mills Press. Reprinted by permission of Peggy Gifford.

THE WONDER OF NATURE
10. **The Delight Song of Tsoai-talee,** N. Scott Momaday. From *In the Presence of the Sun* by N. Scott Momaday. Copyright © 2009 University of New Mexico Press.
11. from **Childe Harold's Pilgrimage,** George Gordon, Lord Byron.
12. **To Look at Any Thing,** John Moffitt. "To Look at Any Thing" from *The Living Seed* by John Moffitt. Copyright © 1961 by John Moffitt, renewed 1989 by Henry Moffitt. Reprinted by permission of Houghton Mifflin Harcourt Publishing Company. All rights reserved.
13. **Perseverance,** Marin Sorescu. *The Biggest Egg in the World* (Bloodaxe Books, 1987).
13. **Manna,** Joseph Stroud. "Manna" from *Of This World: New and Selected Poems.* Copyright © 1998 by Joseph Stroud. Reprinted with the permission of The Permissions Company, Inc., on behalf of Copper Canyon Press, www.coppercanyonpress.org.
14. **Leisure,** W. H. Davies.
15. **Four Haiku,** Kobayashi Issa.
16. **Tiger Got to Hunt,** Kurt Vonnegut.
17. **"Nature" Is What We See,** Emily Dickinson. Reprinted by permission of the publishers and the Trustees of Amherst College from *The Poems of Emily Dickinson,* edited by Thomas H. Johnson, Cambridge, MA: The Belknap Press of Harvard University Press, Copyright © 1951, 1955 by the President and Fellows of Harvard College. Copyright © renewed 1979, 1983 by the President and Fellows of Harvard College. Copyright © 1914, 1918, 1919, 1924, 1929, 1930, 1932, 1935, 1937, 1942, by Martha Dickinson Bianchi. Copyright © 1952, 1957, 1958, 1963, 1965, by Mary L. Hampson.
18. **Return,** Paige Towler. By permission of the author, who controls all rights.
19. **Four Haiku,** Matsuo Basho.
20. **The Morns Are Meeker Than They Were,** Emily Dickinson. Reprinted by permission of the publishers and the Trustees of Amherst College from *The Poems of Emily Dickinson,* edited by Thomas H. Johnson, Cambridge, MA: The Belknap Press of Harvard University Press, Copyright © 1951, 1955 by the President and Fellows of Harvard College. Copyright © renewed 1979, 1983 by the President and Fellows of Harvard College. Copyright © 1914, 1918, 1919, 1924, 1929, 1930, 1932, 1935, 1937, 1942, by Martha Dickinson Bianchi. Copyright © 1952, 1957, 1958, 1963, 1965, by Mary L. Hampson.
21. **The Peace of Wild Things,** Wendell Berry. Copyright © 1998 by Wendell Berry from *The Selected Poems of Wendell Berry.* Reprinted by permission of Counterpoint.

IN THE SKY
24. **Changing of the Guard,** Charles Waters. Reprinted with permission by the author, who controls all rights.
24. from **Night,** William Blake.
25. **Welcome to the Night,** Joyce Sidman. "Welcome to the Night" from *Dark Emperor and Other Poems* by Joyce Sidman. Text copyright © 2010 by Joyce Sidman. Reprinted by permission of Houghton Mifflin Harcourt Publishing Company. All rights reserved.
26. **Old Man Moon,** Aileen Fisher. "Old Man Moon" from *In the Woods, in the Meadow, in the Sky* by Aileen Fisher. Copyright © 1965 Aileen Fisher. Used by permission of Marien Reiner on behalf of the Boulder Public Library Foundation, Inc.
27. **The Man in the Moon,** Billy Collins. "The Man in the Moon" from *Questions About Angels,* by Billy Collins. Copyright © 1991. Reprinted by permission of the University of Pittsburgh Press.
27. **Write About a Radish,** Karla Kuskin. Copyright © 1975, 1980 by Karla Kuskin. Reprinted by permission of Scott Treimel NY.
28. **The Aged Sun,** Anonymous.
29. **Two Falling Flakes,** Douglas Florian. Copyright © Douglas Florian. Reprinted by permission of the author.
30. **Snow,** Edward Thomas.
31. **Looking Through Space,** Aileen Fisher. "Looking Through Space" from *In the Woods, in the Meadow, in the Sky* by Aileen Fisher. Copyright © 1965 Aileen Fisher.

Used by permission of Marien Reiner on behalf of the Boulder Public Library Foundation, Inc.
32. **Night Comes ...,** Beatrice Schenk de Regniers. From *A Bunch of Poems and Verses* by Beatrice Schenk de Regniers. Copyright © 1977 by Beatrice Schenk de Regniers. All rights reserved. Used by permission of Marian Reiner.
32. **A Baby-Sermon,** George Macdonald.
33. **Stars,** A. E. Housman.
33. **When I Heard the Learn'd Astronomer,** Walt Whitman.
34. **The Opposite of a Cloud,** Richard Wilbur. "Poem 22" from *Opposites: Poems and Drawings* by Richard Wilbur. Copyright © 1973, renewed 2001 by Richard Wilbur. Reprinted by permission of Houghton Mifflin Harcourt Publishing Company. All rights reserved.
34. **Rain,** Robert Louis Stevenson.
35. **Windy Nights,** Robert Louis Stevenson.
35. **The Wind,** James Stephens.
36. **The Blue Between,** Kristine O'Connell George. Reprinted with permission by the author, who controls all rights.
37. **Icicles,** Lee Bennett Hopkins. Copyright © 1993 by Lee Bennett Hopkins. Reprinted by permission of Curtis Brown, Ltd.
38. **San Francisco—Any Night,** Kelly Ramsdell Fineman. Copyright © Kelly Ramsdell Fineman. Reprinted with permission of the author.
39. **The Sun and Fog,** Emily Dickinson. Reprinted by permission of the publishers and the Trustees of Amherst College from *The Poems of Emily Dickinson,* edited by Thomas H. Johnson, Cambridge, MA: The Belknap Press of Harvard University Press, Copyright © 1951, 1955 by the President and Fellows of Harvard College. Copyright © renewed 1979, 1983 by the President and Fellows of Harvard College. Copyright © 1914, 1918, 1919, 1924, 1929, 1930, 1932, 1935, 1937, 1942, by Martha Dickinson Bianchi. Copyright © 1952, 1957, 1958, 1963, 1965, by Mary L. Hampson.
39. **This Is My Rock,** David McCord. From *Every Time I Climb a Tree* by David McCord. Copyright © 1952 and renewed © 1980 by David McCord. Used by permission of Little, Brown Books for Young Readers.

IN THE SEA
42. **Tideline,** Kate Coombs. Copyright © Chronicle Books. Reprinted with permission.
42. **By the Sea,** Liz Rosenberg. Copyright © Liz Rosenberg.
43. **At Seacliff Cottage,** Sonya Sones. Copyright © Sonya Sones.
44. **Haiku,** Nick Virgilio. Nicholas A. Virgilio. Reprinted with permission of Anthony Virgilio.
44. **The Negro Speaks of Rivers,** Langston Hughes. "The Negro Speaks of Rivers" from *The Collected Poems of Langston Hughes* by Langston Hughes, edited by Arnold Rampersad with David Roessel, Associate Editor, copyright © 1994 by the Estate of Langston Hughes. Used by permission of Alfred A. Knopf, an imprint of the Knopf Doubleday Publishing Group, a division of Random House LLC and by permission of Harold Ober Associates Incorporated. All rights reserved.
45. **The Mississippi,** Anonymous.
46. **Galápagos: Hood Island,** Bobbi Katz. Copyright © Bobbi Katz. Reprinted by permission of the author.
47. **St. Elmo's Fire,** Georgia Heard. Copyright © Georgia Heard. Reprinted with permission of the author.
47. **Old Man Ocean,** Russell Hoban. Copyright © David Higham Associates. Reprinted with permission.
48. **Bigar Cascade Falls, Romania,** Steven Withrow. Copyright © Steven Withrow. Reprinted by permission of the author.
48. **Flammable Ice Bubbles,** Richard Michelson. Copyright © Richard Michelson. Reprinted by permission of the author.
49. **Lost Giant,** Mariel Bede. Reprinted with permission by the author, who controls all rights.
50. **maggie and milly and molly and may,** E. E. Cummings. "maggie and milly and molly and may" copyright © 1956, 1984, 1991 by the Trustees for the E. E. Cummings Trust, from *Complete Poems: 1904-1962* by E. E. Cummings, edited by George J. Firmage. Used by permission of Liveright Publishing Corporation.
51. **Until I Saw the Sea,** Lilian Moore. From *I Feel the Same Way* by Lilian Moore. Copyright © 1967 Lilian Moore. All rights reserved. Used by permission of Marian Reiner.
51. **What Are Heavy?,** Christina Rossetti.

52. **The Dead Sea,** Rebecca Kai Dotlich. Copyright © 2014 by Rebecca Kai Dotlich. Reprinted by permission of Curtis Brown, Ltd.

53. **Like Ghosts of Eagles,** Robert Francis. Reprinted with permission from *Collected Poems 1936-1976.* Copyright © 1976 by Robert Francis and published by the University of Massachusetts Press.

53. **Ammonites: Sculptures of the Sea,** Betsy Franco. "Ammonites: Sculptures of the Sea," Betsy Franco. Used by permission of the author, who controls all rights, 2014.

54. **Where Go the Boats?,** Robert Louis Stevenson.

54. **The Mill Back Home,** Vern Rutsala. "The Mill Back Home" from *Walking Home From the Icehouse.* Copyright © 1981 by Vern Rutsala. Reprinted with the permission of The Permissions Company, Inc. on behalf of Carnegie Mellon University Press, www.cmu.edu/universitypress.

55. **In the Salt Marsh,** Nancy Willard. "In the Salt Marsh" from *In the Salt Marsh* by Nancy Willard, 2004. Used by permission of Alfred A. Knopf, an imprint of the Knopf Doubleday Publishing Group, a division of Random House LLC. UK rights granted by permission of Nancy Willard in care of the Jean V. Naggar Literary Agency, Inc. (permissions@jvnla.com). Copyright © 2004 by Nancy Willard. All rights reserved.

56. **Take Bus 9 to Red Sea Beach,** John Barr. Copyright © John Barr. Reprinted by permission of the author.

57. **The Red Crabs of Christmas Island,** B. J. Lee. Copyright © B. J. Lee. Reprinted by permission of the author.

58. **The Great Blue Hole,** Donna Marie Merritt. Copyright © Donna Marie Merritt. Reprinted by permission of the author.

59. **I Owe It All to Water,** Mary Lee Hahn. Copyright © Mary Lee Hahn. Reprinted by permission of the author.

ON THE MOVE

62. **Advice for a Frog (Concerning a Crane),** Alice Schertle. "Advice for a Frog," by Alice Schertle, used by permission of the author, who controls all rights.

63. **The Clown Fish,** David Elliot. From *In the Sea.* Text copyright © 2012 by David Elliott. Photographs copyright © 2012 by Holly Meade. Reproduced by permission of the publisher, Candlewick Press, Somerville, MA.

64. **A Blessing,** James Wright. "A Blessing," *The Branch Will Not Break.* Copyright © 1963 by James Wright. Published by Wesleyan University Press. Reprinted by permission of Wesleyan University Press.

66. **The Rhea,** Douglas Florian. "The Rhea" from *Beast Feast: Poems and Paintings* by Douglas Florian. Copyright © 1994 by Douglas Florian. Reprinted by permission of Houghton Mifflin Harcourt Publishing Company. All rights reserved.

67. **Queen Alexandra's Birdwing,** Avis Harley. "Queen Alexandra's Birdwing" by Avis Harley, from *Leap Into Poetry: More ABCs of Poetry,* Wordsong/Boyds Mills Press, 2001. Text copyright © 2001.

67. **Everything Old Becomes New,** Jane Yolen. "Everything Old Becomes New" copyright © 2013 by Jane Yolen. Reprinted by permission of Curtis Brown, Ltd.

68. **Gym on a Rock,** Sonya Sones. Copyright © Sonya Sones.

68. **Electric Eel,** X. J. Kennedy. Copyright © 2014 by X. J. Kennedy. Reprinted by permission of Curtis Brown, Ltd.

69. **On the Grasshopper and Cricket,** John Keats.

70. **The Flower-Fed Buffaloes,** Vachel Lindsay.

71. **The Difference Between Frog and Toad,** Anonymous.

73. **The Ways of Living Things,** Jack Prelutsky. Copyright © Jack Prelutsky. Reprinted with permission of the author.

74. **Quail's Nest,** John Clare.

75. **Self-Pity,** D. H. Lawrence.

75. **Cardinal Nest,** Charles Ghigna. Copyright © Charles Ghigna. Reprinted with permission of the author.

76. **Whale,** Mary Ann Hoberman. "Whale" from *The Llama Who Had No Pajama: 100 Favorite Poems* by Mary Ann Hoberman. Copyright © 1973 by Mary Ann Hoberman. Reprinted by permission of Houghton Mifflin Harcourt Publishing Company and by permission of The Gina Maccoby Literary Agency. All rights reserved.

77. **Sips of Sea,** Avis Harley. From *Sea Stars* by Avis Harley. Copyright © 2006 by Avis Harley. Published by Wordsong, an imprint of Boyds Mills Press. Reprinted by permission.

78. **The Answers,** Robert Clairmont.

79. **Advice from the Scorpion,** J. Patrick Lewis. From *Little Buggers: Insect and Spider Poems,* Dial Books, 1998. Copyright © J. Patrick Lewis, reprinted with permission from the author.

79. **Centipede,** Michael J. Rosen. Copyright © Michael J. Rosen. Reprinted by permission of the author.

79. **The Boa,** Douglas Florian. "The Boa" from *Beast Feast: Poems and Paintings* by Douglas Florian. Copyright © 1994 by Douglas Florian. Reprinted by permission of Houghton Mifflin Harcourt Publishing Company. All rights reserved.

ACROSS THE LAND

82. **You Ask Why,** Li Po.

83. **An Indian Summer Day on the Prairie,** Vachel Lindsay.

83. **To Make a Prairie,** Emily Dickinson.

84. **Afternoon on a Hill,** Edna St. Vincent Millay.

84. **Up on the Hill,** James Hayford. Reprinted with the permission of The New England Press, Inc. Shelburne, VT.

85. **Adlestrop,** Edward Thomas.

86. from **Bat Cave,** Eleanor Wilner. From "Bat Cave" from *Otherwise* by Eleanor Wilner, 1993. Copyright © The University of Chicago Press.

87. **Desert,** Marilyn Singer. Copyright © Marilyn Singer. Reprinted with permission of the author.

88. **At the Un-National Monument Along the Canadian Border,** William Stafford. "At the Un-National Monument Along the Canadian Border" from *Ask Me: 100 Essential Poems.* Copyright © 1975, 2014 by William Stafford and the Estate of William Stafford. Reprinted with the permission of The Permissions Company, Inc. on behalf of Graywolf Press, Minneapolis, Minnesota, www.graywolfpress.org.

88. **Former Barn Lot,** Mark Van Doren. Reprinted with permission from the Estate of Mark Van Doren.

89. **Red Rides West,** Mariel Bede. Reprinted with permission by the author, who controls all rights.

90. **Sailing Stone,** Laura Purdie Salas. Copyright © Laura Purdie Salas. Reprinted with permission of the author.

91. **In a Quiet Dark Place,** David L. Harrison. Copyright © David L. Harrison. Reprinted with permission.

92. **Thank You Note to the Gorge,** Patricia Hubbell. Copyright © 2015 Patricia Hubbell. Used by permission of Marian Reiner for the author.

93. **A Late Walk,** Robert Frost. "A Late Walk" from *The Poetry of Robert Frost,* edited by Edward Connery Lathem. Copyright © 1923, 1934, 1939, 1967, 1969 by Henry Holt and Company, copyright © 1951, 1962 by Robert Frost. Reprinted by permission of Henry Holt and Company, LLC. All rights reserved.

94. **The Song of Wandering Aengus,** William Butler Yeats. Reprinted with permission of A P Watt at United Agents on behalf of Caitríona Yeats.

95. **Nature's Calm,** Alcman. Translated by Edwin Arnold.

95. **The Mountains—Grow Unnoticed,** Emily Dickinson. Reprinted by permission of the publishers and the Trustees of Amherst College from *The Poems of Emily Dickinson,* edited by Thomas H. Johnson, Cambridge, MA: The Belknap Press of Harvard University Press, Copyright © 1951, 1955 by the President and Fellows of Harvard College. Copyright © renewed 1979, 1983 by the President and Fellows of Harvard College. Copyright © 1914, 1918, 1919, 1924, 1929, 1930, 1932, 1935, 1937, 1942, by Martha Dickinson Bianchi. Copyright © 1952, 1957, 1958, 1963, 1965, by Mary L. Hampson.

IN SHADE

98. **Lessons in September,** Tracie Vaughn Zimmer. Copyright © Tracie Vaughn Zimmer. Reprinted with permission.

99. **Time to Plant Trees,** James Hayford. From *Knee-Deep in Blazing Snow: Growing Up in Vermont* by James Hayford. Copyright © 2005 by James Hayford. Published by Wordsong, an imprint of Boyds Mills Press. Reprinted by permission.

100. **Dew,** Charles Ghigna. Copyright © Charles Ghigna. Reprinted with permission of the author.

101. **Butterfly Tree,** Joan Bransfield Graham. Copyright © Joan Bransfield Graham, who controls all rights.

101. **The Monarch's Flight to Mexico,** Avis Harley. Copyright © Avis Harley. Reprinted by permission of the author.

102. **Haiku,** Nick Virgilio. Nicholas A. Virgilio. Reprinted with permission of Anthony Virgilio.

151. **Solar Eclipse,** Steven Withrow. Copyright © Steven Withrow. Reprinted by permission of the author.

151. **Fish Rain,** Marilyn Nelson. Copyright © Marilyn Nelson. Reprinted with permission of the author.

152. **Moeraki Boulders,** Joyce Sidman.

153. **Fossil Beds at the Badlands,** Naomi Shihab Nye. Copyright © Naomi Shihab Nye. Reprinted with permission of the author.

154. **Glacial Erratic,** Helen Frost. Copyright © 2014 by Helen Frost. Reprinted by permission of Curtis Brown, Ltd.

154. **Sun Dogs,** Janet S. Wong. Copyright © Janet Wong. Reprinted with permission of the author.

155. **Catatumbo Lightning,** Kelly Ramsdell Fineman. Copyright © Kelly Ramsdell Fineman. Reprinted with permission of the author.

156. **The Mariana Trench,** X. J. Kennedy. Copyright © X. J. Kennedy. Reprinted by permission of the author.

157. **The Grand Canyon,** Bobbi Katz. "Galápagos: Hood Island" Copyright © 2015 by Bobbi Katz and "The Grand Canyon" Copyright © 2015 by Bobbi Katz.

159. **Mount Everest,** Deborah Chandra. Copyright © Deborah Chandra. Reprinted with permission of the author.

160. **Pink Lake,** Allan Wolf. Copyright © Allan Wolf. Reprinted with permission of the author.

161. **Brinicle,** Laura Purdie Salas. Copyright © Laura Purdie Salas. Reprinted with permission of the author.

162. **Antelope Canyon,** Pat Mora. Copyright © 2014 by Pat Mora. Reprinted by permission of Curtis Brown, Ltd.

163. **Rainforest,** Judith Wright. "Rainforest" from *A Human Pattern: Selected Poems* (ETT Imprint, Sydney 2010), © 1985 Judith Wright. Reprinted with permission.

163. **Niagara Falls,** Avis Harley. Copyright © Avis Harley. Reprinted by permission of the author.

164. **Yellowstone,** Douglas Florian. Copyright © Douglas Florian. Reprinted by permission of the author.

165. **Lake Baikal,** Michael J. Rosen. Copyright © Michael J. Rosen. Reprinted by permission of the author.

166. **Bioluminescence in the Maldives,** Paige Towler. Reprinted with permission of the author, who holds all rights.

166. **Pororoca Tidal Bore,** Janet S. Wong. Copyright © Janet Wong. Reprinted with permission of the author.

167. **Wonder Down Under,** Ted Scheu. Copyright © Ted Scheu. Reprinted with permission of the author.

168. **Red Tide,** April Halprin Wayland. Copyright © 2014 by April Halprin Wayland. Reproduced by permission of the author.

169. **Petrified Forest,** Amy Ludwig VanDerwater. Copyright © 2014 by Amy Ludwig VanDerwater. Reprinted by permission of Curtis Brown, Ltd.

170. **Aurora Borealis,** Steven Withrow. Copyright © Steven Withrow. Reprinted by permission of the author.

171. **Northern Lights,** J. Patrick Lewis. Copyright © J. Patrick Lewis. Reprinted with permission of the author.

LAST THOUGHTS
172. **Nothing Gold Can Stay,** Robert Frost. "Nothing Gold Can Stay" from *The Poetry of Robert Frost*, edited by Edward Connery Lathem. Copyright © 1923, 1934, 1939, 1967, 1969 by Henry Holt and Company, copyright © 1951, 1962 by Robert Frost. Reprinted by permission of Henry Holt and Company, LLC. All rights reserved.

173. **Nature,** Henry David Thoreau.

174. **Swift Things Are Beautiful,** Elizabeth Coatsworth. Copyright © Bethlehem Books. Reprinted with permission.

175. **Lessons of Nature,** J. Patrick Lewis. Copyright © J. Patrick Lewis. Reprinted with permission of the author.

176. **the earth is a living thing,** Lucille Clifton. "the earth is a living thing" from *The Book of Light.* Copyright © 1993 by Lucille Clifton. Reprinted with the permission of The Permissions Company, Inc. on behalf of Copper Canyon Press, www.coppercanyonpress.org.

177. **In Beauty May I Walk,** Anonymous (Navajo Indian)

178-179. **Post-it Notes From the World,** J. Patrick Lewis. Copyright © J. Patrick Lewis. Reprinted with permission of the author.

Back cover, **Astoundingly Breathtaking Creation,** Carole Weatherford. Copyright © Carole Boston Weatherford. Reprinted with permission.

Cover, Eric Baccega/naturepl.com; back, Solvin Zankl/naturepl.com; case front, Dennis Kirkland/Jaynes Gallery/DanitaDelimont.com; case back, Johanna Phillips Huuva/Shutterstock; flap, courtesy of J. Patrick Lewis; all painted watercolor backgrounds throughout: Shutterstock; 4-5, Tobias Helbig/Vetta/Getty Images; 6-7, NASA; 8-9, Hidehiko Sakashita/Flickr RF/Getty Images; 10-11, Charles Gurche; 12, SolangeB Photographie/Flickr Open/Getty Images; 13, Charles Gurche; 14, Charles Gurche; 15, Igor Siwanowicz/Visuals Unlimited/Corbis; 16, Steve Winter/National Geographic Creative; 17, Lori Epstein/National Geographic Creative; 18, Jeff Mauritzen; 19, Visuals Unlimited/Corbis; 20, daffodilred/Shutterstock; 21, Nikographer [Jon]/Flickr RM/Getty Images; 22-23, Kemmud Sudsakorn/Moment Open/Getty Images; 24, Charles Gurche; 25, kelly bowden/Flickr RM/Getty Images; 26-27, Peter Komka/epa/Corbis; 28, Chase Swift/Corbis; 29, Jeff Mauritzen; 30, jonathan sloane/Vetta/Getty Images; 31, NASA; 32-33, Michael Durham/Minden Pictures; 34, Charles Gurche; 34 (LO), Dmitry Naumov/Shutterstock; 35, Maria itina/Moment Open/Getty Images; 36, Annette Kiesow; 37, David Ponton/Natural Selection/Design Pics/Getty Images; 38-39, Ropelato Photography/EarthScapes/Flickr RF/Getty Images; 40-41, Luciano Candisani/Minden Pictures; 42-43, Justin Horrocks/iStockphoto; 44, George Grall/National Geographic Creative; 44-45, Carl M Christensen/Flickr RF/Getty Images; 46, Michael Melford/National Geographic Creative; 47, Auke Holwerda/E+/Getty Images; 48, Porojnicu Stelian/Shutterstock; 48-49, LaiQuocAnh/Shutterstock; 49, Chris Johns/National Geographic Creative; 50-51, Chris Newbert/Minden Pictures; 52, Michael Melford/National Geographic Creative; 53, Charles Gurche; 53 (LO), alicephoto/Shutterstock; 54, Lori Epstein/www.loriepstein.com; 55, James P. Blair/National Geographic Creative; 56, Wang Song/Xinhua Press/Corbis; 57, Jurgen Freund/NPL/Minden Pictures; 58, Paul Nicklen/National Geographic Creative; 60, Tim Fitzharris; 62, Joel Sartore/National Geographic Creative; 63, Stephen Frink/Digital Vision; 64, Johann S. Karlsson/Flickr RF/Getty Images; 66, Nancy Rose/Flickr RF/Getty Images; 67, FranÁois Gilson/Biosphoto; 68 (UP), forest71/Shutterstock; 68 (LO), Norbert Wu/Minden Pictures; 69, Gemina Garland-Lewis; 70, Tim Fitzharris; 71, Tim Fitzharris; 72, FloridaStock/Shutterstock; 74-75, GreenArt Photography/Shutterstock; 76, Flip Nicklin/National Geographic Creative; 77, Fred Bavendam/Minden Pictures; 78, Vikulin/Shutterstock; 79, cellistka/Shutterstock; 80, Charles Gurche; 82, Carr Clifton/Minden Pictures; 83, Annie Griffiths/National Geographic Creative; 84, Charles Gurche; 86, Joel Sartore/National Geographic Creative; 87, Angel Di Bilio/National Geographic Your Shot; 88, Sinelyov/Shutterstock; 89, Steve Byrne; 90, Ropelato Photography/EarthScapes/Flickr RF/Getty Images; 91, Charles Gurche; 92, Aimin Tang/Stockbyte/Getty Images; 93, imagedepotpro/E+/Getty Images; 94, Charles Gurche; 96-97, Leroy Francis/Hemis.fr RM/Getty Images; 98-99, James A. Guilliam/Photolibrary RM/Getty Images; 100, Paul Zahl/National Geographic Creative; 101, Joel Sartore/National Geographic Creative; 102, Roger Brandt/National Geographic Your Shot; 103, Michael Nichols/National Geographic Creative; 104, Sebastian Kennerknecht/Minden Pictures; 105, MilousSK/Shutterstock; 106, Joel Sartore/National Geographic Creative; 107, Charles Gurche; 108 (UP), Daniela Duncan/Flickr Open/Getty Images; 108 (LO), Suppavut Varutbangkul/Shutterstock; 109 (UP), Hannele Lahti/National Geographic Creative; 109 (LO), Amy Neunsinger/The Image Bank/Getty Images; 110, Craig Hale/E+/Getty Images; 111 (UP), Dr. Morley Read/Shutterstock; 111, mauritius images GmbH/Alamy; 112, Gay Bumgarner/Photographer's Choice/Getty Images; 113, Mitch Diamond/Photodisc/Getty Images; 114, Dieter Schaefer/Flickr Open/Getty Images; 115, Richard Williams/National Geographic Your Shot; 116, Pete Oxford/Minden Pictures; 117, Ken Canning/iStockphoto; 118-119, NASA; 120, Matthias Breiter/Minden Pictures; 121, Art Wolfe/The Image Bank/Getty Images; 122-123, Sadatsugu Tomizawa/AFP/Getty Images; 124, Ken M Johns/Photo Researchers RM/Getty Images; 125, shaunl/Vetta/Getty Images; 126, Hougaard Malan/Riser/Getty Images; 127, Cultura Science/Jason Persoff Stormdoctor/Stone Sub/Getty Images; 129, Mike Hill/Alamy; 130, Mark Thiessen/National Geographic Creative; 131, Sharon Day/Shutterstock; 132-133, magdasmith/E+/Getty Images; 134, Scott Leslie/Minden Pictures; 135, Zigzag Mountain Art/Alamy; 136, Charles Gurche; 137, Shinji Kusano/Nature Production/Minden Pictures; 138, Varts/Shutterstock; 139, Lisa Couldwell/Flickr RF/Getty Images; 140, Stefano Stefani/Photographer's Choice RF/Getty Images; 141, Jordi Strijdhorst/Buiten-beeld/Minden Pictures; 142 (UP), Mm-photos/Photodisc/Getty Images; 142, Charles Gurche; 143, Foto Polimanti Fabio/Flickr RF/Getty Images; 144-145, LOOK/Getty Images; 146-147, Ingo Arndt/Minden Pictures; 148, Jean-Paul Ferrero/Auscape/Minden Pictures; 149, Mike Hollingshead/Corbis; 150, Angela Carr/Atom Ray Photography; 151, James P. Blair/National Geographic Creative; 152, Khoroshunova Olga/Shutterstock; 153, TC Yuen/Flickr Open/Getty Images; 154 (UP), Loop Images Ltd/Alamy; 154 (LO), isarescheewin/Shutterstock; 155, Tourism Ministry/Xinhua/Alamy Live News/Alamy; 156, Mark Thiessen/National Geographic Creative; 157, Michael Nichols/National Geographic Creative; 158, Alex Treadway/National Geographic Creative; 160, Jean-Paul Ferrero/Auscape/Minden Pictures; 161, Nature Picture Library/Alamy; 162, Charles Gurche; 163 (UP), Piotr Naskrecki/Minden Pictures; 163 (LO), Robert Harding Picture Library Ltd/Alamy; 164, Tim Fitzharris; 165, Nutexzles/Flickr RF/Getty Images; 166, Doug Perrine/naturepl.com; 167, Simon Bradfield/iStockphoto; 168, Alexander S. Kunz/Flickr RF/Getty Images; 169, Yva Momatiuk & John Eastcott/Minden Pictures; 170-171, SurangaSL/Shutterstock; 172, Tracy Jenkins/National Geographic Your Shot; 175, Samantha Nicol Art Photography/Flickr RF/Getty Images; 176-177, Celso Mollo Photography/Moment Open/Getty Images; 178-179, Zoran Ivanovich/iStockphoto; 180, jps/Shutterstock; 182, Stephen Belcher/Minden Pictures

Staff for this Book
Jennifer Emmett, Paige Towler, *Project Editors*; Lori Epstein, *Senior Photo Editor*; Amanda Larsen, *Art Director and Designer*; Rachel Kenny, Sanjida Rashid, *Design Production Assistants*; Colm McKeveny, *Rights Clearance Specialist*; Grace Hill, *Managing Editor*; Joan Gossett, *Senior Production Editor*; Natalie Turner, *Rights Clearance*; Alyson Foster; *Research Specialist*; Lewis R. Bassford, *Production Manager*; Jennifer Hoff, *Manager, Production Services*; Rahsaan Jackson, Imaging; Susan Borke, *Legal and Business Affairs*

The National Geographic Society is one of the world's largest nonprofit scientific and educational organizations. Founded in 1888 to "increase and diffuse geographic knowledge," the Society's mission is to inspire people to care about the planet. It reaches more than 400 million people worldwide each month through its official journal, *National Geographic,* and other magazines; National Geographic Channel; television documentaries; music; radio; films; books; DVDs; maps; exhibitions; live events; school publishing programs; interactive media; and merchandise. National Geographic has funded more than 10,000 scientific research, conservation, and exploration projects and supports an education program promoting geographic literacy.

For more information, please visit nationalgeographic.com, call 1-800-NGS LINE (647-5463), or write to the following address:

National Geographic Society
1145 17th Street N.W.
Washington, D.C. 20036-4688 U.S.A.

Visit us online at nationalgeographic.com/books

For librarians and teachers: ngchildrensbooks.org

More for kids from National Geographic: kids.nationalgeographic.com

For information about special discounts for bulk purchases, please contact National Geographic Books Special Sales: ngspecsales@ngs.org

For rights or permissions inquiries, please contact National Geographic Books Subsidiary Rights: ngbookrights@ngs.org

Hardcover ISBN: 978-1-4263-2094-1
Reinforced Library Binding ISBN: 978-1-4263-2095-8

Printed in China
15/PPS/1

Acknowledgments
To the entire National Geographic team for their enthusiasm and dedication in the making of this book, and to all the poets whose deserving work, regrettably, could not be squeezed into its pages. —JPL

The publisher gratefully acknowledges the heroic efforts of Natalie Turner in securing permissions, as well as the invaluable research assistance of Alyson Foster.